THE CATHOLIC SEEKER'S JOURNEY

My Journey Into the Catholic World

Why Did I Convert to Catholicism?

Andrew Jordan, III

Copyright © 2016 Andrew Jordan

All rights reserved. No part(s) of this book may be reproduced, distributed or transmitted in any form, or by any means, or stored in a database or retrieval systems without prior expressed written permission of the author of this book.

ISBN: 978-1-62217-801-8

Acknowledgements

I wish to thank the employees at Saint Anthony Book Store in Greenville, South Carolina, for recommending that I pursue Catholicism. I'd like to thank Fr. Dwight Longenecker for recommending his book, *More Christianity*, for me to read. I'd like to thank my parish priest Father Patrick Tuttle and some of the members of Saint Anthony Church of Padua for helping me through the RCIA process, and for not giving up on me through my struggle with embracing Catholicism. I'd like to thank the EWTN crew in Birmingham, Alabama, especially Father Joseph [Mary] for motivating me to remain Catholic after my first confession with him. I would like to give a special thanks to Noah Lett for introducing me to some of the EWTN staff, who took me on a tour around the studio. I'd like to thank Noah Lett of EWTN for sharing his conversion experience with me and for recommending some Catholic resources to me. He did not know how much he blessed me when I met him on my pilgrimage through EWTN in 2013. I went to Steubenville, Ohio, in 2015, on a special trip to see and thank Scott Hahn personally. I told Scott Hahn at the bible conference, after he signed his book that I'd bought, how he'd impacted my decision to convert to Catholicism. I would like to thank Scott Hahn for inspiring me to become Catholic through his teachings on EWTN.

Contents

Acknowledgements... iii
Introduction..1
Chapter One
One Universal Spiritual Family..7
Chapter Two
Catholicism Misunderstood 13
Chapter Three
The Journey for Answers & Discernment 23
Chapter Four
Sacred Symbols, not Pagan Symbols 31
Chapter Five
Mary, Our Blessed Mother 41
Chapter Six
The Seat of Saint Peter..49
Chapter Seven
Catholicism is Christianity 59
Chapter Eight
Trinitarian Godhead..65
Chapter Nine
The Mass: Christ's Presence 73
Chapter Ten
The Day of Confirmation...81

Chapter Eleven
Call to Separation 87
Chapter Twelve
Catholic Mediations & Acts of Contrition 91
Chapter Thirteen
Catholic Enlightenment 115
Chapter Fourteen
Vocational Discernment 129
Chapter Fifteen
Urgent Evangelization from Within 137
Chapter Sixteen
Catholic Cultural Shock 145
Bibliography 160

Introduction

My whole entire mission and purpose for writing this book is because some non-Catholics have misconceptions about Catholicism. Before I became Catholic, I had misconstrued ideas about Catholicism because I was taught that Catholicism was a pagan religion. Believe me, there are some prejudices against Catholics, yet some have respect for the Catholic faith.

Did I agree with everything Catholicism teaches? I agree that it is the True Spiritual Church because she has maintained the apostolic tradition. Externally the Church does not always agree on things, like any other Church, not when it comes to some externalities, but the internal aspect, which is the soul of it, I agree with wholeheartedly. The same goes for the Protestants. Each denomination or sect, including Catholicism, made claims to have been the truth faith. It's like reading a billboard sign on the highway that advertises a business that brags and claims to be best in town or in the state. Although that slogan claims to be better than its competitors, it does not mean that the business always delivers.

I spoke mostly subjectively as well as objectively, but I was revealing what Catholicism taught as objective truth. One must have respect for objective truth and objective authority, but both do not dictate the soul or the conscience. God has ordained the leaders of the Church to inform the moral conscience and convict the soul through the Holy Spirit.

I have been a Baptist-Evangelical all my life, yet open to different Christian faiths. I am now a Catholic. I am a Catholic-Evangelical because

I grew up on the Protestant side of the fence, and I still adhere to some of the core fundamental principles of the faith. Paul was a Jew to the Jew and a Gentile to the Gentile (1 Corinthians 9:19-20). His ministry was to the Gentiles, but he never stopped being a Jew. The Jews, in his time, did not consider him a Jew once he converted to Christianity. However, I have not stopped being an Evangelical. I no longer am a Baptist by practice or label. I could defend the Catholic side of the fence because I have been a follower of it for five years. Its fundamental core truths are the same. Christianity as a whole shared these axioms of Biblical teachings. I want us to examine the basics of the Catholic faith. As a Catholic, I am still wet behind the ears, and I also have a whole lot of growing to do. As a theologian and as a minister of the word, I will always have a need for spiritual growth and insight. I admit that I am not a Catholic apologist or an Evangelical apologist. I am not an expert on Catholicism, but I do know the fundamental truths of the Christian faith enough to adapt to any form of theology. My intentions are not to throw judgment on either group. The goal is to find common ground, as well as clarity. My objective is to embark on a journey for the truth and insight in my spiritual walk.

I am not trying to syncretize the Christian faiths because I have learned how to respect each entity without knocking them. We Christians can learn to appreciate the knowledge of God in each of them. After all, we are a spiritual body made up of many members. I have learned that Catholicism is not for everybody. It means that God has us where he wants us to be, but this does not mean that we cannot embark on a spiritual journey by becoming open-minded to the other Christian religious schools of thought. It is sad to say that many groups who are not Catholic are afraid to examine a faith without being afraid of it. At first, I was scared of Catholicism because I was ignorant of the faith.

Once I learned to examine her soul (Catholicism), I then began to understand her true essence. One cannot judge a faith by its followers, but one can judge a faith on its principles and vision. Therefore, my whole point is to never judge a book by its cover.

I have called this book The Catholic Seeker's Journey because I wanted to share my journey and conversion experiences with both Catholics and non-Catholics. The ultimate questions are: "Why Did I become a Catholic?" and "What finally convinced me to become Catholic?" The last question meant that I struggled for almost three years before becoming a Catholic. There were several theological obstacles that I faced during my RCIA (Rite Christian Initiation for Adults) process. It was the Holy Spirit who helped me overcome the theological obstacles. God led me to Catholicism. He directed me to the faith, according to His purpose.

We are not only called to serve God, but we are also called to cultivation. We as Catholics and Protestants are called to become what God has called us to become, and that is to "Be Holy!" because God is Holy. The believer's salvation is through the journey toward the prize. God matures us through the process. Although we were saved by the grace of God, we're also justified by faith, according to the righteousness of God. Our salvation is a lifelong process.

Catholicism taught that final salvation comes to the believer at the time of death. Paul told the Church of Philippi to work out their own salvation with fear and trembling, not through human merits, but through the spiritual cultivation process under the work of the Holy Spirit (Philippians 2:12). We cannot get from A to Z without going through the process in between. I was born Baptist, raised Baptist, and was a licensed Baptist minister. Each phase for me was God's way of cultivating me. Catholicism was not the end in itself, but it served as the means to the "crown of life" that God has in store for me. The steps of a good man are ordered (Psalm 37:23). Why fight the call, when we can flow with the call? If I had remained in the Baptist Church, I would have missed out on the knowledge treasures that God had in store for me, not because the Baptist denomination was a false faith, which it was not, but because I would have become complacent in my walk and become dormant. I had to move. Sometimes I wondered if I had made the right move by becoming Catholic. Every time I thought about going back, God had ways to keep me from turning back. Every one of us has to come face to face with crossroads. I have definitely been faced with life and religious crossroads.

I went from the Jehovah's Witnesses to the Pentecostal movement, to the Reformed Movement, and finally to Catholicism. The journey began externally and then later became internal. John 8:38 says: "And you shall know the truth, and the truth shall make you free." I sought for purpose and meaning. That was what the Catholic journey was all about for me. Rejections that I had faced earlier in life led me to embark on this spiritual journey. Despite what I had in mind, God had something else in mind.

The Catholic Seeker's Journey is not only about searching for the truth. It is also about what the journey taught me — how to fight the internal war within my soul. Augustine and I had a lot in common. We were both young and in pursuit of meaning, yet we both had two opposite backgrounds. Like Saint Augustine's journey to the truth, I went through a similar thing, except his was far more intellectual. Augustine admitted that his will was in battle. Augustine fought with the carnal desires from within, and strived to be pure.[1] Before and after confirmation, my soul was in turmoil. I believe what folks say about digging too deep: "The deeper one goes, but the harder it is to come out." Augustine found that

---

[1] Tom Gill. Confessions, Saint Augustine. (Gainesville, FL: Bridge-Logos, 2003). 205,207

true happiness led him to God. He also realized that God was the source of true happiness.[2] I sought the truth so that I could find happiness. The truth was there all along, but I was too blind to see it. So when one searches far and wide and never finds what he or she is looking for, then the only place one can look is within his or her soul. The believer has the Spirit of God within himself or herself. The Spirit of God is the Revealer of Truth. Since he is the Revealer of Truth, access to understanding is granted to all of us. We, as God's people, are not only heirs, but family as well. The secrets of the kingdom are revealed to us through divine revelation (Matthew 13:11). Therefore, the Spirit reveals the deep things of God, which the world cannot understand, because Christ's wisdom is foolish to them (1 Corinthians 1:27-30; 2:6-10).

---

2 Ibid., 277,278

Chapter One
One Universal Spiritual Family

FAMILY CONSISTS OF MEMBERS OF one household. Catholics see themselves as one big family. I did not say "one big happy family." Catholics do not exclude other Christians because all are one family. There is division in the family, yet she is still family. Christ is our peace, who has made us one, and who has broken down the middle wall of separation. Christ came to put away enmity through the cross (Ephesians 2:16). Some Protestants, especially many Evangelicals, beg to differ. Family members do not always agree with one another on some things, but it does not mean that the members are no longer family. The same can be about the spirit realm. The Church is universal. The blood of Christ runs through the Church's veins because his blood is life of the body, just as life of the flesh is in the blood. We are bone of His (Jesus's) bone, and flesh of His flesh, and are one flesh (Genesis 2:23-24, 29:14; Mark 10:6-8; and Ephesians 5:31). Jesus said, "So then, they are no longer two but one flesh. Therefore what God has joined together, let no man separate" (Matthew 19:5-6, NKJV). Paul wrote: "But he who is joined to the Lord is one spirit with Him" (1 Corinthians 6:17, NKJV). Paul spoke of marriage as the Great Mystery between Christ and his Church, according to John Paul II. Pope John Paul II wrote that life, according to the Spirit, expresses itself also in the reciprocal union or knowledge. It is a vocational call.[3]

---

3 Michael Waldstein's Introduction John Paul II. Man and Woman He Created Them, A Theology of the Body. (Boston, MA: Pauline Books Media, 2006). (Di-

The point is that all Christians bear the mark of the spousal love of Christ and the Church. Since all Christians, in spite of the labels we give ourselves, are already baptized, which is the entry of God's people, the entry is a nuptial mystery.[4]

Catholicism teaches that marriage is a sacrament that applies to both the natural and the spiritual. Marriage is a permanent seal between the spouses (husband and wife). It is designed to be an unbreakable bond between husband and wife. Marriage is not perfect, yet it remains one in relations between two people. Christ is our head (husband), and we (body) are his bride. Since we Protestants, Evangelicals, Catholics, and Jews were knitted together as one, we are to grow as one (Ephesians 2:21). We are called to walk in the unity since Christ gave himself for his Church. According to John Paul II, marriage has to come into reality, which is beyond contract. Marriage is reality which is "in sickness and in health, in joy, in sorrow, and love and to honor all the days of my life." The only way we can have a consummated marriage is through conjugal intercourse.[5]

The word catholic means universal, in the sense of "according to the totality" or "in keeping with the whole." "The Church is catholic because Christ is present in her."[6] True, there is a difference between the terms catholic and Catholic. The capitalized word Catholic refers to the Roman Catholic Church. Some non-Catholics have less of a problem with the spiritual catholic Church. Definitely, the term Roman Catholic is a huge deal. Many Christians, who are not Catholic by label, believe that Catholicism is not a Christian faith, but pagan Romanism. Before and

---

mensions of Covenant and Grace, sacrament and "Redemption of the Body," 101:6, General Audience Dec. 1, 1982). 523

4 CCC. (Catechism of the Catholic Church, Liberia Editrice Vaticana, 1994, 1997 Paragraph 1617).404.

5 CCC. Paragraph 103:2. The Dimension of Sign, "Language of the Body" and the Reality of the Sign, General Audience of January 5, 1983). 532.

6 CCC. Article 830

after the Reformation, many Christian sects disassociated themselves from Catholicism by attempting to purge Christ's Church of Roman Catholicism. There are radical groups who wanted to return to the Church's roots. There are so-called radical Christian movements today that want to return to the ways of the early Church, during the era of the Apostles. Each denomination has had founding forefathers, whose ideology has been to redefine Christ's Church.

Catholicism does claim to be the true faith, so do all Christian sects. Catholicism never claimed to have been a perfect faith. Its teachings and beliefs were centered on Jesus Christ.

The Church has always had schisms since the beginning of the early Church era. Paul wrote to churches, which had factions, like Corinth. There were movements within the Church itself. Here is my point! The Church was and still is the Church, no matter what name we give our assemblies, if she (the Church) belongs to Christ. Why do we treat one another like foreigners when we are no longer foreigners (Ephesians 2:19)? Let us go back to our grassroots!

The Church is definitely apostolic, pertaining to administration and order. The Church is definitely spiritual. The Church's roots are Judaic. There were some groups that I have encountered that believed that the Apostle Paul was the author of the division because of the split between the Jews and Gentiles. If Orthodox Christianity claims to be pro-Paul, then it really needs to re-examine the Pauline epistles. Paul wrote to the churches concerning the issues that divided the churches during his day. The modern-day churches are repeating the same thing.

The letters to the Ephesians and to the Galatians are both excellent starting points. I learned, under my New Testament professors, that the split was mainly over law, salvation and circumcision. Legalism was the major division in the Church of Galatia. Cultural division was among the Church of Ephesus. Paul wrote that there were no distinctions in the spiritual body of Christ, in regards to one's ethnic identity, social status, or gender. Paul also wrote that it was Christ's blood that reconciled us to God the Father. Christ's ultimate goal was to make one new man.

Why don't Catholics label themselves as Christians? I was told that there were too many labels among Christian groups. Many groups identify themselves as whatever group they belonged to. This does not mean that these groups are not Christians. Catholic was not the first term used by believers. The term catholic is one of the earliest labels the Church used all the way back to the early second century. Jesus did not use the term Christian anywhere in the gospels. Even the Jewish sects label themselves according to their movements, yet they all were Jews by faith and culture. Jesus never prohibited religious labels, but he only objected to the sects' hypocrisies. What Jesus would object to are not the religious labels in Christianity, but to the hypocrisy and the enmity that exists in his body, consisting of members. Unfortunately, there are inconsistencies among Christian groups. Since we have been engrafted into the olive tree as branches belonging to the family of God, we are one in faith, mind, and baptism under the new covenant (Romans 11:17, Ephesians 4:5). If we are one big spiritual family, why aren't we one big happy family? Protestants and Catholics have repeated what the early Jews and Gentiles had already done. Paul wanted the two groups to bury the Hatfields' and the McCoys' feud.

If Catholics are not Christians, then neither are the Protestants because the Protestants are the daughters of the Mother Church (Catholicism), no matter how much Protestants deny this claim. The Church needs a constant reminder on Christ's purpose for coming into the world. Jesus came, not only just to give us life, but to also bring us into perfect unity and love. His love for us, through His suffering, was to put away the enmity between the two groups (Ephesians 2:12-17). The Holy Spirit operates through the Catholic Church, as well as the Protestant churches. Catholicism does believe that the Spirit of God operates in all churches, except the sects do not have the entire fullness of God. Catholics refer to Protestants as separated brethren. At first, I thought Catholicism taught that Protestants were not true Christians since Catholicism claims to have maintained the apostolic tradition. Catholicism claims to be the true faith and the only faith that taught the whole truth. In essence, it is a true faith. This meant that the core or the soul of the faith was true. I raised questions about the external aspect because many of her practices were Roman-centric in custom and tradition. Jesus said that "a tree is known by its fruits." Catholic deeds, therefore, speak for themselves. I will let the readers decide for themselves. All I ask is that one research the Catholic faith through open lenses, rather than through Protestant lenses. We are the extensions of the Jewish faith because we were engrafted into the family of Abraham through Christ (Romans 11). We were adopted into the family of God, like it or not. All who believe in the Lord Jesus Christ, according to faith, are of the family of Abraham. The Holy Spirit has sealed the children of God through Jesus Christ, his only begotten son (2 Corinthians 5:5).

Paul wrote that we are one body made up of many members from every ethnic and social status. In Christ, there are no distinctions. We are one. Although we have different disciplines and different sect labels, we are still one body. The gifts of the Spirit were given to one body, his spiritual body (1 Corinthians 12). The family is like a human body. It consists of many members, but it shares one purpose. Jesus prayed that his disciples would be one (John 17). We are a living organism. The family is, therefore, a breathing entity. Apostle Peter said: "Coming to Him as to a living stone, rejected indeed by men, but chosen by God and precious, you also, as living stones, are built up a spiritual house, a holy priesthood …." (1 Peter 2:4-5, NKJV). Apostle Paul said "One

Lord, One Faith, One Baptism, One God" (Ephesians 4:6). The true worshippers, whether Catholics or Protestants, are to worship God in spirit and in truth.

Chapter Two
Catholicism Misunderstood

Facts and Misconceptions about Catholicism and Catholics

MANY NON-CATHOLICS BELIEVE THAT CATHOLICS do not believe and teach the Bible because Catholics have their own version of the Bible (the Douay Version) rather than the King James Version.

Here is my response to the statement: Catholicism does teach the Bible. In fact the entire liturgy in the Catholic Church is saturated with Scriptures. I have to say, since I became a Catholic, I have hardly seen a Catholic carry around a Bible with him or her. True, many Catholics do not read or know their Bible like some Protestants do, but many Protestants do not read their Bible either. Many Evangelical denominations read the passages of Scripture from the pulpit to their congregations during worship and have outlines like Catholicism does. I am referring to the order of worship. Catholicism teaches its followers from the Catholic Catechism. Reformed Churches do have their own creeds and confessions, yet each one believed that the creeds and confessions were only aids, and they did not replace the Absolute (Infallible) Authority (word of God). Catholicism is the opposite. Evangelicals did have far more Bible studies, verse by verse, with their members than Catholics. Catholics do have Bible studies, but not in the same manner as Evangelicals and Reformers do. Although I was new to the Catholic Faith, I grew up in Protestant and Evangelical circles all my life, and I have seen the differences between the two groups. I admit that there are Bible deficiencies within both groups.

I have talked with some former cradle-Catholics who told me that Catholics never taught them the Bible. When these former Catholics became Protestants, these former Catholics seemed to become more Bible literate and anti-Catholic. I believe that the Church (Mother Church) teaches and preaches from the Scriptures and according to Apostolic Tradition. Here was one problem I had with Catholicism on the topic of Scripture. The Church needed not only to inform the conscience of the people, but she needed to expose its members more to the Scriptures. More Catholics ought to read the Scriptures for themselves, yet Catholics are to adhere to the objective norms of the Church. It is possible, but hard to do. Slowly Catholics are beginning to read the Bible more, yet still adhere to the interpretation of the Church. Catholicism believes: "Apostles left Bishops as successors 'handing over' to them 'the Authority to teach in their own place.' Authentic interpreting the word of God entrusted to them the living truth of the office of the Church. The teaching office is not above the word of God, but serves it, teaching only what has been handed on."[7] Later I understood why Catholic clergy did not allow the common people access to the Scriptures before and during the time of the Reformation. Luther, Wycliffe, Huss, Tyndale, and Zwingli had good intentions of cleansing the Church of its abuses and corruptions. When it came to Scripture, there were pros and cons that came out of the Reformation. The pros were that the lay people needed to be taught the word of God. The Reformers believed that the word of God alone would quicken the spirit of the people, and open the lay people's eyes to God's truth. After all, the Scriptures make wise

---

[7] Vatican II, Dei Verbum. Dogmatic Constitution on Divine Revelation, Pope Paul IV Nov. 18, 1965, Para. 10 verse 12. (Online)

unto salvation (1 Timothy 2:15-16). The Church did control the masses by keeping them ignorant from the word. The cons were that the seeds of division and heresy rose up out of the Reformation Movement. The Roman Catholic Church knew that private interpretation would lead to not only chaos, but disunity, both politically and spiritually. Later, I understood why Catholicism rejected Sola Scriptura.

Scripture Alone! There were tens of thousands of sects, denominations, and non-denominational groups that were the result of the Protestant Reformation. Some non-Catholics believe that they do not need a priest, but can go directly to God for themselves. On the contrary, these groups did not deny the need for pastors and preachers to interpret the Scriptures for them.

Jesus said, "Man shall not live by bread alone, but by every word that proceeded from the mouth of God" (Matthew 4:4, King James Version). The whole point that I made in this statement was that, since some non-Catholics believe that Catholics do not read the Bible, their conclusions are that Catholics do not know the truth about Jesus Christ and that Catholics are being deceived by the Roman Catholic Church. I know this because I thought the same way as a Protestant-Evangelical. This leads to statement number 2.

Catholics are not saved because Catholics worship Mary and the Pope, but not Jesus Christ. Catholics need Evangelization (preaching the Gospel from Scripture,) and to accept Jesus Christ as their Lord and Savior (Romans 9:10). Catholics are lost to Jesus Christ.

I admit that, throughout my observation and Catholic journey, I observed many Catholics lacking Scripture. I did not lack Scripture learning because I was trained all my life through the Bible. Some Catholics know their catechisms better than I do because it has been part of the routine for cradle-Catholics. First of all, I know, for a fact, that Mary is not the center of the Catholic Faith, and Mary definitely has never been the object of worship. Jesus Christ is the center of the Catholic faith as he is in the Christian sects. Jesus is glorified throughout the entire liturgy of the Catholic faith. Second, Catholics have never worshiped the Pope. However, Catholics acknowledged the Pope as the head of the Church in the administration sense, but not in place of Jesus Christ, who is the Head of the Church spiritually. If a Catholic worships the Pope or Mary, then that Catholic is totally ignorant and blind to his or her faith (see the topic on Mary and the Papacy).All my life I've heard sermons preached in pulpits that say people are to come to the altar and accept Jesus Christ as their personal Lord and Savior. I have no objection to this because Jesus is the only way to salvation and to the Heavenly Father.

Many Evangelicals would be out on the streets and behind podiums preaching salvation. These were the famous statements that I heard all my life: "Do you know the Lord?", "Are you saved?" and "Have you received the Holy Ghost and spoken in tongues?" What does it mean "to know the Lord?" "Knowing the Lord" is not in the abstract sense (intellect), but in the prudent and marital sense. Knowing God and Jesus Christ is covenantal. Adam knew his wife Eve. Adam declared Eve "bone of his bones and flesh of my flesh" (Genesis 2:23). Enoch walked with God. Evangelicals were right to ask the question, but hardly anyone was able to explain "knowing the Lord." Most Catholics have a very good understanding of what is means to "know the Lord." Knowing the Lord is covenantal for a Catholic.

Salvation is through the Church (Mother Church) because she is the ground and pillar of truth. The Church is to inform the conscience to the gospel through instruction. Some people would say that we do not need a church to be saved. I used to think in this manner until the Spirit showed me. The answer is found in the Letter of Romans. In Romans 9, it asks, how can a person be saved without a preacher? The lost need a preacher in order to respond to the gospel. Faith comes by hearing. One cannot believe in what he or she has not heard. All churches have to agree that all Christian institutions and leaders are guardians of God's flock. Here is the God's honest truth! The Catholic and Protestant Churches need to be evangelized from within. How can we give an answer to our faith, if we do not know our faith? God is my judge and not man. God is sovereign, and He does whatever He pleases (Psalm 115:1). He shows mercy upon whomever He desires to show mercy upon (Exodus 33:19, Romans 9:18).

Catholics are not Christians because Catholics believe in works and righteousness through human merit and through indulgences and penance.

The myth is that many non-Catholics believe that Catholics do not know the Lord because Catholics merit their salvation through mere works alone. It is true that Catholics do not teach Sola Gratia (Grace Alone). Grace is primary because no man can be saved apart from the grace of God. It was through the love and merit of Jesus Christ on the cross. All Christianity and Catholics agree on this. Grace is followed by faith and works (the seven sacraments of the Catholic Faith). It is true that Catholics do not teach Sola Fide (Faith Alone) because it does not say faith alone in Romans and James, according to Catholicism and the Bible. Romans does say that we were justified by faith and not by works (mere human merits). The just do live by faith, but it does not say "faith alone." The truth is that Catholics believe that faith and works coincide with one another, like the body and soul does, according to the letter of James. Catholicism's core teachings are from James. What did Paul and James mean by "works"? The works both men were speaking of were charitable acts or external deeds that would not bestow freedom upon the individual. Virtues are attributes that are to be expressed, not as a means for salvation, but as virtues that are to be expressed through the salvation that was given to us through Jesus Christ. No man can see God without holiness (Hebrews 12:14). Holiness is not a work, but the nature of God. Being Holy is not a work, but a nature we must become (1 Peter 1:16, Leviticus 20:26).

Does attending a Catholic Church assure salvation? "Outside the Church there is no salvation..,"[8]

What does this mean? True, Catholicism believes that the Church is the place where salvation is taught. A person can receive Jesus Christ through any Christian institute that teaches the core truths of the Christian faith. Catholicism has not objection to this, except Catholicism believes that she teaches the whole fullness of God since the denominations broke away from the Church. Sects taught limited truths, according to the Catholic priests that I have personally talked to.

In fact, denominations claimed to have taught the absolute truth and that people should go to Church to be saved. When I was growing up, I heard old folks say that if we did not go to Church, we would go to hell. Many of us felt that we were forced to go to Church on Sundays. Were the old folks right? "The Church is the pillar and ground of truth" (1 Timothy 3:15).

The Church is to teach the whole truth of salvation without holding back. We as Christians and Catholics with a full knowledge of God's word cannot detach ourselves from the body spiritually, or we can and will spiritually die by disconnecting ourselves from God. We are not to leave

---

8 CCC. Article 845

any sheep out. It is our mission to go after the scattered sheep. "To unite all his children, scattered and led astray by sin, the Father willed to call the whole of humanity together into his Son's Church. The Church is the place where humanity must rediscover its unity and salvation. The Church is 'the world reconciled.'"[9] Do Catholics believe that other religions can be saved without ever learning and hearing about Jesus Christ? "This affirmation is not aimed at those who, through no fault of their own, do not know Christ and his Church."[10]

I grew up in a church setting that taught that all who have not heard and know the Lord will go to hell because Jesus said that he is "the Truth, the Way and the Life, and that no man comes to the Father except through him" (John 14). There were Christian groups that taught that there is no way to heaven, except through the gospel. My father debated my mother, who was pastor at the time, and some of his friends that were pastors and ministers on his job about those who did not hear about Jesus long before Jesus came on the scene. What about the people before Jesus's time who never heard of Jesus Christ? In the Old Testament era, not all people heard of the God of Abraham. This is a valid argument. The Catholic priests told me that, as long as there is no fault on their own, there is a possibility that they could be saved. This is also in the Catechism of the Catholic Church. Who really knows except God Himself? Even two-thirds of the world has not yet heard and received the gospel. If their governments forbid the gospel to be preached, then what are we to expect? A lot of effort has been put into getting the gospel to these people as we approach the second coming of Jesus Christ.

Some Non-Catholics believe that Catholicism teaches that salvation comes through the forgiveness of sins through a priest and through the purchase of indulgences to get loved ones out of purgatory.

---

9 CCC. Article 845-846
10 CCC, Article 847

Here is my response: The priests serve as Christ's mediators between the Church body and Christ as the head. Priests and bishops are God's representatives on earth. Priests are intercessors, like pastors in local churches, and serve as mediators between God and their parishioners. True, there is only one mediator between God and man, who is Jesus Christ.

At first, I struggled with confessing to a priest. Some sins are so personal that no one wants to share his or her deepest secrets and sinful passions with a priest without being judged. The priest keeps confessions confidential. Some are ashamed to open up their personal skeletons. I learned that there are venial sins and mortal sins. Venial sins are recent sins that can be repented of before they continue to go on un-repented. Mortal sins are grave sins that we never repented of in our lifetimes. Engaging in mortal sin can be an unforgivable sin in this life and the life to come. Mortal sin can mean one who totally and deliberately rejected the invitation to salvation.

Purgatory is not hell; instead it is a place where believers can deal with the personal sins that they never repented of. Purgatory is a painful process of fire purging before entering heaven. In the Protestant canon, there is no Biblical support for such doctrine as purgatory or praying for the dead. Catholicism does make one point. Without holiness, no man can see God. This made me think and rethink about purgatory. I somewhat believed it, but I needed more Biblical evidence for the claim for the doctrine of purgatory. I could meet middle ground on this topic because the Holy Spirit is to present the Church before Christ without spot or blemish. The purging does not take place when we get in heaven. The Spirit purges the Church on earth before she is taken to heaven. Jesus will present His bride without spot or blemish. There has to be something taking place between death and heaven, if there is immediate life after death with absolute certainty. Purgatory is hard to understand, and it is controversial. Jesus said, "If thy right hand offends thee, cut it off. It is better for one of the members to perish, than for the whole body to be destroyed in hell. If thy right eye offends thee, pluck it out. It is better for one member to perish than the whole body to be destroyed in hell" (Matthew 5:29-30, NKJV). I was taught through the Wesleyan Theological School of Thought that entire sanctification takes place between departing this life into the next. We know that sanctification has to take place in this life. Sanctification is not merited but is the cleansing work of the Holy Spirit.

Chapter Three
The Journey for Answers & Discernment

IT IS TRUE THAT CURIOSITY usually leads to something. My curiosities about Catholicism led me to confirmation and conversion to the Catholic faith. I went three rounds through the RCIA. The third round was the charm. The third round was filled with many inner obstacles inside my interior soul. Protestant-Evangelical convictions and my conscience were the obstacles I battled with on the journey. Jesus told His disciples that they did not choose Him, but rather He chose them. Earlier I mentioned, in the introduction, that Catholicism was not for everybody. Just as everyone is not fit for the kingdom of heaven, the same is for any faith. I met a former Protestant, who I considered a brother in the faith, in Conyers, Georgia, who told me this. I have cherished this word of confirmation since then. Jesus said: "Many are called, but few are chosen" (Matthew 22:14, NKJV). This does not mean that the invitation is not offered to the non-chosen because it is an act of free choice, rather than by force, through the Spirit. The first two RCIAs were interesting, but I dropped out within the earlier part of the course. My disillusions with denominations led me not to remain in the Baptist or Evangelical movements. I felt compelled to pursue Catholicism.

    A Catholic woman told me that I would better understand the faith by being inside rather than seeing it from the outside without bias. A fellow Catholic sister, not a nun, helped me through the journey. She encouraged me to buy a book on spiritual discernment. I was taught in the charismatic circles that the gift of discernment meant discerning spirits that were either from God or not, or by seeing into the spirit realm in the charismatic sense. Discernment is not an ecstatic or sensational feeling. There are some who have the supernatural gift to discern spirits. The sister explained to me that the gift of discernment meant knowing the perfect will of God. Seeking God meant longing for the Righteousness of God (Matthew 6:33).

That was Paul's prayer and encouragement to the churches (Romans 12:2). I prayed to God for the gift of discernment, and God did give me the gift of discernment. The heavy dark veil of fear began to lift up off me slowly as I approached the Easter Vigil. In the beginning, I felt that I did not belong in the Catholic family because there were some who made feel me uncomfortable, who treated me as an outsider. Even after the conversion, some of the Catholics Some Catholic churches I visited made me feel a sense of unwelcome, and some Catholic churches made me feel welcome. There were times I was paranoid because I experienced hurt in the past from different Churches, especially the non-Catholic churches. A non-Catholic friend told me if I hold on to the pains of the past afflicted by some churches, then will feel out of place wherever I go. I spent three years praying and meditating so that I could forgive and move on. I felt that the faith helped me to find sanity. Catholics embraced me as a brother and as a fellow-believer.

I became a Catholic under rejection and hurt pretenses. I was looking for, not only the truth, but a place of acceptance. I felt out of place in the denominations, especially the Baptist churches as a minister. I felt that my knowledge and religious education were either too much or not enough. There were some who felt threatened by my theological education. , I became very frustrated with trying to share the things that I had learned in seminary. I felt that my gift was not needed to benefit the body. So I began to question my faith and my calling into the ministry.

The more rejection I received, the more I grew weary, and I became almost disillusioned with churches. It was not the principles of the faith that almost turned me away but the hypocrisy, the racism, and the social classism and cliquish attitude within the walls of Churches. It was not so much people rejecting the person Jesus Christ. Many reject how people represent him. I knew that the grass was not greener on the other side. When my father passed and my mother retired, I began to sink into a dark place where the enemy (Satan) was constantly attacking my mind and soul. I tried to go through other denominations, but these groups did not open their arms to me. Mom always told me that people could be mean and nasty everywhere I went. I saw the worst case scenarios in the some churches than I did in my home church. The sole reason that I left the Baptist denomination and my home church was because I felt that there were too many limitations. I knew that I had to expand my horizons. I was ready for innovative learning. I felt that many of the churches were not ready to learn theology and deep church history. I encountered members some Christian groups who knocked theology and attending seminary because both were not "spiritual." Jesus said that a prophet is without honor in his home country. I had to leave Galilee or Nazareth, in the figurative sense, in order to embark on my journey, which was the high calling, (Matthew 13:57, Mark 6:4).

Catholicism loves sharing theological ideas and beliefs without disputing. What I mean is that many Catholics find interest in other beliefs with the former Protestants' experiences because the Catholic faith believes that there is knowledge of God in all of them, except that the denominations have part of the truth. when it comes to the fullness of God's presence Catholicism believes that she is the only faith that teaches and have the whole truth. Neither the Protestants nor Catholics do not embrace relativism. Relativism believes that there is no absolute truth. People can have different views about morality and immorality.

Cultures and interpret morality in according to subjective views. This philosophy holds no one accountable. On the contrary, the Church becomes the moral conscience to the people. The Church holds people accountable for their own actions. Neither person is wrong. Christianity teaches the absolute truth. The Church is the pillar and ground of truth, (2 Timothy 3:14). I am not a relativist, but I do believe in absolute truth. The word of God is absolute truth. No Church is all-knowing. Only God is all-knowing. Human beings are finite creatures. God has the absolute truth. God has to feed us a little at a time, or we will choke on the word. Taking in the whole truth all at one time is too much to attain. Every Church lacks something, and I am sorry to say it. ; I would be lying if I did not say so. Paul said that t we know and prophesy in part. Now we see only a reflection as in a mirror, and we shall see Him face to face. Then we shall know fully, (1 Corinthians 13:9-12). God allowed me to incorporate His truth from the different sects into my personal faith, yet I learned to respect each Church entity separately.

Call me the Seeker. Andrew the Apostle was a seeker, and Jesus's first disciple. I was seeking purpose rather than identity. My faith has to center on God. I have learned that it's not only me and the Lord, but Christ and his body. The journey enabled me to embark on journey where I could discover my purpose. A seeker has many questions. A seeker is longing for meaning, and someone greater than him or herself. I left the Baptist Church. I learned to set aside those things that would hold me back. I took nothing on my journey. I loved Jesus more than anything or anyone. I placed Jesus Christ as top priority.

I was ready for the deep things of God, and I knew that I would only gained so much through the sects of Protestantism. The sects were not enough. I knew that I would only get fragments of the truth. I had a philosophy and belief in broadening my horizons. I did not believe in confinement when it came to the truth and knowledge. I learned to think outside the box. The box is only a form of control. I could subject to religious authority. I would not let religious authority dictate my thinking or faith. I learned this from my previous religious experiences.)

I am using the ocean analogy. Catholicism is a like an ocean filled with knowledge. Although oceans have boundaries, the waters are very deep. There are hidden treasures within deep waters. I learned to swim in deeper waters. Catholicism has in exhaustive knowledge. In exhaustive knowledge presented challenges to me. Knowledge is a lifelong, ongoing thing.

Philosophy is not evil in itself, but it is inadequate if it is being used to save the souls of individuals. Philosophy is not liberation, but rather curiosity. The world's philosophy is vain philosophy that results in vice, but divine wisdom makes one wise unto salvation through the Holy Spirit (Colossians 2:12). No personal or man-made theologies and philosophies will surpass revelation. Revelation is God's self-disclosure to the Church. The Spirit of God is the Revealer of Truth; it convicts the human heart of sin and is the Amender of human hearts and minds of men. I learned from Thomas Aquinas that reason cannot be neglected. A human cannot deny his human makeup. Mankind cannot be moral without reason. God is Mind and Intellect as well as Spirit. Reason through the guidance of revelation keeps mankind from being barbaric. God gave us the ability to reason, but reason must be guided by divine revelation. Reason cannot replace faith. I learned to infuse faith and reason in my journey, but I still seek revelation. My parish priest made an interesting statement in the RCIA class. My priest said, "Revelation is not new. It has been around for centuries. Revelation was constantly repeated throughout time but through different individuals." In other words, revelation cannot be added or subtracted, rather it circulates in history cycles through eras.

God has opened my eyes throughout my spiritual journey by revealing himself to me piece by piece. One thing about me was that

I never deprived myself of access. For years, God enabled me to go to places that had much access, but none of the places that I went to were like the Catholic Church. There was an elderly Catholic woman at the bookstore, who encouraged me to pursue Catholicism. Catholicism, she said, was a large ocean filled with truths. Since then, I have fallen in love with Catholicism.

I believe that God saved me from apostasy. Apostasy was far more difficult than I thought. I learned never to underestimate the root of one's faith. I could not easily drift away because of the truths and the word of God instilled in me since childhood. God led me to the Catholic Church. My intentions were not to join but to receive clarity in purpose and in spiritual direction. I always longed for God's revelation. I began to read the Catholic Catechism on the Church. Catholicism made it clear to me that, for one to go against the Church, is for one to go against God. Christ chose Peter as the chief Apostle that would establish order and administration. It was through the Church that salvation was proclaimed. Although the Church did not always behave as the Church, she was God's design. The Church is the "Bride of Christ." Christ, who is the Head, sacrificed Himself for His bride. I remembered the story of Jonah when God called Jonah to preach and prophesy to Nineveth. Instead, the Prophet Jonah ran from his calling, attempting to sail to Tarsus. God frustrated his plans by causing the storm to stir up the sea. Jonah was tossed off the ship into the belly of the fish for three days. During the three days in the belly of the fish, he repented and went to fulfill the call that God placed upon him (Book of Jonah).

God called Abraham to become a "father of many nations." Moreover, Abraham had to go through tests and journey toward his calling. Abraham was a sojourner. He and his family wandered from place to place without ever settling. Journeys are restless, but journeys are the means of cultivating and maturing saints. God chose Moses to deliver the Hebrews out of Egypt. Before the Hebrews could inherit the Promised Land, the Hebrews had to sojourn out from Egypt to Mount Sinai for forty years before entering Canaan. Therefore, the growth is in the journey, not in the destination.

Catholicism was the means to the blessings God had in store for me. I went from Baptist to Catholic. The steps of the righteous were ordered by God. I thank God for allowing me to be raised as an Evangelical because my Baptist Evangelical roots provided me with a Biblical foundation. I was raised by a female minister. I was taught by an elderly woman who was a minster and a scholar to recite verses in her Bible study group. I thanked the Jehovah's Witnesses for giving me the zeal to search for the truth. Sometimes I regretted going to Bible college and seminary because I felt that I would never use it. However, it enabled me to pursue the truth, the meaning, and the purpose. One phase set me up for the next phase, and these all led me to my Catholic journey. I knew this was God's plan for me.

Chapter Four
Sacred Symbols, not Pagan Symbols

THERE ARE MANY NON-CATHOLICS WHO believe that not only Roman Catholicism is a cult, but also a pagan religion because of its icons and symbols. True, there are parallelisms in both Christianity and other religions. Remember Satan is a duplicator who distorted the truth into a lie. Catholicism attacks Dan Brown's so-called fictional The DaVinci Code, which says that Christianity derived from paganism. Emperor Constantine worshiped the sun-god and instituted sun-worshipping in the Roman Empire. Constantine mingled the Jesus sect and the pagan sects into a "hybrid religion." Christianity was, therefore, believed to have been pagan.[11] This was very convincing because there was whole lot of truth to the history of Christianity. The faith was not pagan, but pagan terminologies and concepts did creep in, not during Constantine's reign, but all the way back to the apostles' time. The apostles fought to keep heresy and pagan idolatry out of the Church. Most of the Early Church Fathers, before 325 AD, were Pagans and philosophers before converting to the faith. Later, the Apostolic Fathers became defenders of the Christian Faith against heretics and Pagans.

There were critics, who were anti-Christian, who slandered the religion of Christianity. I have watched YouTube videos about Christianity being satanic. The faith was of the Babylonian religion. During the time of

---

11 Mark Shea. *The Da Vinci Deception*. (West Chester, PA: Ascension Press, 2006). 111-113

the apostles, there were schisms and factions in the body of Christ. The first split was between the Jews and Gentiles. The Church went from Jewish to becoming more and more Gentile. The Jewish sects separated themselves from the Christian sects due to persecutions in the Roman Empire against Christians who refused to pay tribute to the Roman emperors. I had to do a paper on Domitian when I took a course on Revelation in seminary. The Church was under heavy duty persecution and suffering. As the Church became more Gentile, idolatry, philosophy, and sexual immorality crept in. The Church was Euro-centric because the Church was influenced by the Greco-Roman customs. European customs were placed upon the whole Christian world through the Roman Church. Catholicism claimed to have held on to the Jewish feasts and customs; the Church was seen as being far from Jewish in practice, even the denominations did not have any Jewish flavor in them. Many Christian groups begged to differ on the Catholic Church continuation of the Hebrew tradition. I sat under a Jewish apostle who taught that the Christian religion was pagan and satanic.

Unfortunately, there was a lot of truth in what he taught. The Church became tainted with Gentile concepts and customs. I have been in Jewish synagogues, and they were totally different from the Churches. The Jehovah's Witnesses taught me something similar. I have read black liberal theologians such as Albert Cleage and James Cone who taught the "Black Theology of Liberation." Jesus was black or that "God is black." African-Americans were believed to have been part of a systematic oppression of Eurocentric Christianity. I questioned it for several years.

When I was a Baptist minister, I volunteered with my church group to minister at the prison facilities every third Sunday. I have encountered some Black Muslims who argued with me that Christianity was a "white man's" religion, which has been used as a means of controlling masses of people. I was told this by black disciples of black cults and prison inmates. Even some atheists and liberals argued with me that Christianity was a means to suppress people of knowledge and truth. Eurocentric Christianity had feudal systems in them. Classism was in the Christian Roman Empire. The Mother Church was indeed political. Many factions like the Donatists had a problem with the political Roman Catholic Church because of her complacency in power. I remembered doing a paper on the "Donatists Schism" Saint Augustine course. Augustine was the defender of the Mother Church against Pelagians, the Manicheans, and the Donatists. The Mother Church was the sanctioned Church in the empire that claimed to have held the apostolic tradition.

Icons, Relics, and Saints

Catholics use the word sacrament that derives from the Latin word sacramentum, which is translated from the Greek word mysterion. It means an efficacious symbol. The symbols were very special in Catholicism. It was a concrete reality that, in some way, it was what it represented. In other words, the symbols point to another reality.[12] While I was in seminary I took a course on "worship." The seminary was centered on Reformed Calvin Theology. The professor took the class to a huge Presbyterian Church in Greenwood, South Carolina. The students were to observe and critique the building's sanctuary. This sanctuary was unlike any I had seen before in my whole life. There were no drawings or images on the windows. One could see outside from the sanctuary. The outside view was a scenic setting. It seemed like a quiet place of meditation. I learned through this field trip that God taught His people revelation, even through nature. There were not any relics, just a scenic view.

---

12 Michael Pennock. This is Our Faith, A Catholic Catechism for adults. (Norte Dame IN:Ave Maria Press, 1998). 102

Author's source from CCC 774-776,780.

There was a Catholic church in downtown Greenville, South Carolina, that had a mausoleum memorial and a walkway with green grass and flowers. The sanctuary was filled with art on the stain glass windows, altars with incense, etc. Symbols were used to explain spiritual truths. Hindus, Buddhists, Muslims, and even some Jews make pilgrimages. Catholics make pilgrimages, as well. Some non-Catholics call it idolatry. I've heard it from some of my Protestant friends. Going to a shrine or a pilgrimage is not sinful. It is no different than going to the Holy Land (Jerusalem), Greece, Rome, or Orlando, Florida, to the Holy Land Experience. Why can't Catholics do the same? Why do some non-Catholics make a big deal about shrines and relics? It is a personal journey and experience. It is all about spiritual enlightenment. I went to Hanceville and Birmingham, Alabama, on a spiritual pilgrimage. The studio in Birmingham and the shrine in Hanceville were filled with history and the art of martyrs, saints, and renowned doctors of the Church, although these were statues. What was unique about the tour was that each symbol had a story behind it. I had a New Testament professor who told the class that religion was attracting. Catholicism was very attracting but in a good way. Symbols explain the spiritual aspect or significance. A Church without symbols would seem to be empty.

When a Catholic enters a sanctuary, the first thing that he or she does is the sign of the cross. Then, he or she will kneel, facing the altar, as a sign of reverence and respect. Anything in place of God is an idol, even worshipping symbols. Some Protestants view reverencing saints as idolatry.

Catholics do not worship icons or consider icons to be gods. It would be very foolish to worship icons since icons have no life or power in them. The Old Testament prohibited Israel from worshiping idols. The idols do not have any magical powers to them. Idols are harmless in themselves. There is no life or power in icons because there is no life in them. We have to be careful not to become superstitious.

Protestant or Catholic, humans need symbols to understand spiritual truths that we cannot understand through human reasoning. Symbols cannot replace divine revelation. Catholicism used many symbols, not for the objects to be worshiped, but to teach its members. Symbols served as reminders for those who served God in the past saints.

Prayer to the Saints

In the beginning, I really struggled with this issue of the saints. Praying to the saints was definitely controversial to many non-Catholics. I struggled with life after death, immediate transition between death and heaven. There was no actual proof, other than Jesus returning from the dead in a matter of days, not after a few hours or resuscitation. Who really knows if the people are in heaven or hell? I could not go on one's near death experience as evidence, or someone who claimed to have gone to heaven or hell and come back. I have talked to people who have actually died and returned and had no such experiences. This made me question what happens to life immediately after death. We all agree that Jesus will return and resurrect the dead in Christ, the first-fruits. I have had Catholics tell me that heaven is more of God's presence, rather than a place. Again one has to be conscious, and the soul, not the body, has to know where it is.

I tried to avoid teachings on life after death because we have not yet experienced it. One cannot prove or disprove one's experience. For a while, I left it alone. I was certain of the miracles performed through saints such as Francis of Assisi, Anthony, Giovanni, Saint Patrick of Ireland, Padre Pio and others. Praying to saints was uncertain because I'd never had an apparition or vision of a saint appearing to me, like Sister Maria Faustina Kowalska, Padre Pio, Damien, Catherine of Sierra, or the Our Lady of Fatima, where Mary was supposed to have appeared.

Before the election of candidates for RCIA confirmation, we had to choose a saint name. I thought about Athanasius or Augustine because these men were apologetic defenders of the Church, but God gave me Francis of Assisi. I related to him the best because he was seen as odd and different. I did not need an intellectual saint; instead, I needed a saint with humility. Apostle Andrew was one of my choices because my name is Andrew, and Andrew was a seeker and a defender, but I felt that I was not worthy to take on him as my saint because he was martyred. I do have an icon of Apostle Andrew to serve as a reminder of my personal struggles in my spiritual journey. When I was a Protestant, I understood that the apostle's creed is part of the "communion of saints," as just the gathering of God's people in fellowship. In Catholicism, it's communion with the saints that have gone on to be with the Lord. There are tons of saints who are believed to have gone on to be with God. Catholics do not pray to dead saints because the saints are in heaven. If the saints are dead, then I have a major question about after death transition. I admitted immediate life after death was always an issue for me since the Jehovah's Witnesses taught me about how the dead sleeps until the day of resurrection. I struggled, at first, with the prayer to the saints for intercession. How do we know that the saints are not praying for us? How do we know that our deceased loved ones are not praying for us? Angels pray for us. Michael is our prince and guardian who is always making intercession for Christ's Church (Jude 9). There were many images of saints in the Catholic Churches, not pagan symbols that drew evil spirits. The saints, according to Catholicism, serve as intercessors. At first, I had some questions about the revering of the saints because the Bible does not mention it. If we go on Scripture alone, then the Protestants would have a case. A couple of Catholic priests used an illustration about the picture of a love one who has died, which serves as a reminder. Sometimes a person talks to a loved one as if that person were still alive. I talk to my father sometimes at home with his picture in front of me. Washington D.C. is full of icons, but they serve as reminders, not as gods. It is believed by some that our national symbols have some pagan origin or background, although the nation was founded upon Biblical principles. Non-Catholics would say that is different, but it really is not. Leaders do not pray to icons, but to God immemorial around the icons. I talked to my saint, Francis of Assisi, a whole lot. I do not have to necessarily pray to Saint Francis or Mary or any saint. Jesus is our true Intercessor, according to the canon of Scripture. Protestants say that Jesus is the only Mediator between God and man (1Timothy 2:5). Catholics say that Jesus is the Intercessor and Mediator between God and man, and Mary intercedes specifically for the Church through Jesus Christ.

The word mediator in the letter to Timothy from Paul was referring to sacrifice. Mary was never the sacrifice, but Jesus was the Lamb who was slain for the ransom of many. Jesus is the Mediator of the new covenant by means of death (Hebrews 9:15).

Intercession is not worship, but the intercession serves as a channel where grace is conveyed to the world through the Church (I Corinthians 12). In the Old Testament, the Levitical priesthood interceded for the nation of Israel before God in the tabernacle. Since Jesus lives and serves as the Eternal High Priest, according to Melchizedek, we can directly go to him, according to faith (Hebrews 7:24-25). However, the people need visible representatives to stand before God on their behalf, and the Church serves as the visible representatives on earth.

Some Protestant Churches use symbols, but not as much as Catholic Churches. The cross is the object that symbolizes the Christian faith, rather than being just a cross or a crucifix. In pagan religions, crosses were used to ward off evil spirits. The Kingdom Hall rejected steeples and crosses because crosses were used in pagan cults. Catholics and some Reformed churches do the "sign of the cross." As a former Baptist, I thought the sign of the cross was a vain ritual conjured up by the Roman Church. Methodist and Episcopalian students did it in the preaching class. I never understood why they did it. I did think the "sign of the cross" was Biblical, but it was revealed to me that the angels placed a tau or a cross on their foreheads as a sign of protection from destruction (Ezekiel 9:4). I have done the sign of the cross all the time since then, even during my private devotional time with God. Ezekiel 9 was the Catholic argument for the sign of the cross. The Crucifix was not a mere symbol for Catholics, but a sacred reminder of Christ's death to those who were still experiencing suffering in this world. No, the crucifix is not re-sacrificing Jesus over and over on the cross. Catholics believe in the resurrection of Jesus Christ. Jesus said to celebrate his death. "Do this in remembrance of me" (Luke 22:19). His death served as a reminder of why he sacrificed his life for us. Catholics never worshiped the crucifix. The crucifix was a sacred symbol, not a rabbit's foot or a superstitious good luck charm.

What I was taught in Church History classes were mostly true. Roman paganism only switched partners. In pagan Rome, the emperors were revered, even Constantine and his successors erected icons of themselves until Justinian broke the tradition by erecting the first huge icon of Jesus over the main gate called the Bronze Gate at Constantinople (685-95 A.D.).[13] Emperor Leo III (717-41) launched an attack on the use of icons. His motivation to do away with icons was believed to have been done through guilt since Christianity taught against pagan idolatry. Emperor Leo III grew up near the Arab frontier. He was very influenced by Islamic teachings. Those who had icons were persecuted. There was a debate over the use of icons. The emperor ordered that the icon of

---

13 Tim Doley. <u>Introduction to the History of Christianity</u>. (Minneapolis, MN: Fortress Press, 1995). 256

Christ over the bronze gate be replaced with a cross.[14] Islam accused Christianity during the crusades of idolatry because of its graven images. God punished Israel for idolatry. It was John of Damascus who defended the icon of Jesus. The Old Testament warned Israel not to worship other gods and make graven images (Exodus 20:2-3). The Word did not become flesh yet. So the Father remained invisible (Deuteronomy 6:4). In the New Testament, the Word became flesh. Now we have an image, not a mere image, but the God-man, Jesus Christ (John 1:14).

---

14 Ibid. 257

Chapter Five
Mary, Our Blessed Mother

I WAS AFRAID, AT FIRST, of the Catholic faith because the relics and Hollywood version of Catholicism had given it a bad name. I met former cradle-Catholics who told me that the Catholic faith was pagan. True, Mary was described as theotokos (God-bearer). I was taught that Catholics worshiped Mary as the Madonna and as a Goddess. The term Madonna was a medieval term for noble or first lady, a woman of importance, especially in reference to Mary. In French, it is Notre Dame (Our Lady). When Catholics call her Madonna, they are not calling her a goddess. The image or icon of Madonna holding the baby Jesus serves as a representation of Mary.[15] Saints were considered dulia (veneration, honor, respect). Mary was considered hyperdulia (special honor or veneration). It is believed that Mary is venerated in the place of the goddess Diana and that Catholics do not worship Jesus Christ. This is far from the truth. I have observed the mass and the liturgy of the Catholic Church with my own eyes. Catholicism is the opposite of what I had been taught. Even though Mary played a major role in salvation because she conceived the Incarnate Son of God, she is not the redeemer. One priest said: "Mary is not another redeemer or another mediator. Instead she works with her Son for the redemption of the world. She mediates with Christ for the salvation of souls. As such, she is a model

---

15 Wikipedia Free Encyclopedia. www.wikipedia.com.

of what we should be doing."[16] Grace was, therefore, in her womb. Mary was in no way divine, and she was not of the Trinity. She was honored, and she was given a special position with her Son.

It seemed that pagan cultures and religions had similarities. Where did these accounts come from? There was some element of truths in pagan mythologies. This was no coincidence. My personal research brought me to a point where I questioned the origin religion of Christianity? I was taught this under the Jehovah's Witnesses. I was convinced until I attended Bible college. That was when a red flag rose up in me, and I began to ask questions. True, there were pagan accounts on immaculate conceptions a virgin births. The Immaculate Conception meant that Mary's life was without original sin, another word for ancestral sin. The term original sin was derived from Saint Augustine. She was believed to have been born without sin because the Spirit of God shielded her from original sin, and Mary's birth was not miraculous like Jesus's birth.

Mary was born through both parents, according to the Proto-Evangelium of James. Catholicism believes that Mary maintained her virginity. My priest actually mentioned this in the RCIA. He also told the class that Augustus Caesar was born immaculately as the embodiment of the Roman Government. This, I never knew. A Protestant would counter this doctrine by saying that Mary acknowledged that she, too, needed a Savior. Mary was a virgin when she bore the Son of God. Both parties agree. There was some objection in the Early Church on Mary's perpetual virginity, especially from Tertullian. Saint Jerome and Augustine defended Mary's perpetual virginity. Catholics always pray to her, but they have never worshiped her. Mary was venerated. I did not like the word venerate because the Roman Emperors, during the Christian persecution era, were "venerated" as gods on earth. Honor would be the appropriate word rather

---

16 Dwight Longenecker. More Christianity. (Huntington, IN: Our Sunday Visitor Publishing Division, 2002). 218

than venerate. The theological terms did have pagan origins behind them. We all know that Greco-Roman culture was pagan.

I grew up only hearing about Mary during the Christmas holidays. Protestants agreed that Mary was a virgin when she conceived the Son. Jesus was born without intercourse because he was conceived by the Holy Spirit. All parties agree on the virgin birth of Jesus, but not on Mary's Immaculate Conception and Mary's perpetual virginity. I have to admit that, at first, Catholics did seem to overemphasize Mary by placing her high on the pedestal. Yes, Mary was honored and full of grace and highly favored among women. Blessed was the fruit of her womb who was Jesus (Luke 1). This was recited in the Rosary. The Queen aspect was controversial (Revelation 12). Dispensational groups debate if the "woman" was Israel or the Church. Catholicism argued that it was Mary who was believed to be crowned with twelve stars. Scott Hahn's book Hail Holy Queen made me think about Mary as the woman spoken of in Revelation, as well as in the Second Eve. Jesus said, "Woman, behold your Son." Gebirah was the Hebrew word for Queen Mother. It was a high and special position for the queen. It was carried out through the David Dynasty and the nine tribes of Israel, especially in the line of Judah.

Jeremiah spoke of the crown of the Queen Mother (29:2; 13:18). Sarah was given this title (Genesis 16:4, 8-9; 1 Kings 11:19). Egyptian queens were called Queen Mother. No, Mary's position was not derived from the goddess Isis (1 Kings 15, 33; 2 Kings 5:3, 10:13. The Wedding in Cana raised a red flag in the back of my mind (John 2:5). Both Irenaeus and Tertullian supported Eve as a type or shadow of Mary. Irenaeus argued: "Thus the knot of Eve's disobedience was loosed by the obedience of Mary. What the virgin Eve had bound in unbelief, the Virgin Mary loosed through faith." Irenaeus also said: "So also Mary, betrothed to a man but nevertheless still a virgin, being obedient, was made cause of salvation for herself and for the whole human race."[17] Catholics seemed to have a stronger case for Mary as the woman. Mary was compared to Queen Bethsheba, who was the mother of King Solomon. Bethsheba always pleaded before King Solomon on the behalf of a person (1 Kings 1:16-17, 31). True, the queens, such as Queen Esther and Queen Bethsheba, stepped in as intercessors before their kings on behalf of their citizens.

The only New Testament account that was recorded was the wedding at Cana. In ancient Israel, the queen was not a mere figurehead. Rather, she held an office with real authority in the kingdom.[18] Catholicism used Jeremiah's prophecy to justify the argument. Mary knew that her Son was destined for greatness. She knew his time had come. She had to beg to Jesus and move Jesus to do what he was called to do. It was obvious that Mary and Jesus had a deep relationship. Mary was with her Son from His birth until His death and resurrection and ascension. Even on the cross, Jesus requested the Apostle John, rather than her biological children, which was believed by some to take care of His mother. Catholicism has a point because why John and not one of her sons?

The early Church fathers argued in their writings that Eve was a type of Mary. Eve was deceived by the fallen angel (Satan), while Mary was obedient to the voice of the angel (Gabriel). Catholicism's argument was that Mary never had children after Jesus was born, but most Protestants disagree because the gospels mention Jesus having brothers and sisters. Either Jesus had brothers or sisters believed to have been from Joseph's previous marriage or Mary had more children after Jesus.

---

17 93. St Irenaeus, Against the Heresies, Article 224
18 86 Leon J. Suprenant. <u>Catholic for a Reason II, Scripture and the Mystery of the Mother of God</u>. (Steubenville, OH:Emmaus Road Publishing, 2000)

I tried to get a couple of Catholic priests to respond to the non-Catholic's argument against Mary being the co-mediator with Christ because there is no real Biblical support for the case of praying to Mary. Catholic priests explained the Immaculate Conception and the virtues of Mary as the spiritual model, which I embraced, because she conceived the Son in a pure state. Mary was not incapable of sinning, but she was protected by the Holy Spirit since birth. I agreed with Mary's perpetual virginity. Praying to Mary was an issue for me because the scriptures clearly teach that not only should we pray to the Father, but the Son is the Mediator between God and man. Catholics do pray to God the Father, and the Son. In the back of my mind, I embraced it to a certain degree maybe because I did not fully understand the Rosary. I knew this for a fact, but during the Rosary, Catholics prayed to Mary during their own devotional time. Catholicism is often accused of vain worship, empty babbling words, and vain repetitions. The prayers are recitations, not vain repetitions. There are some Catholics who, like some Protestants, worship mindlessly. It is really up to the individual how he or she devotes his or life in prayer, mediation, and devotion through faith. During the Mass, Jesus was the center of worship, and Mary was hardly mentioned. She was not, in any way, portrayed as divine. I have to give Catholicism her props. Catholics were not ashamed to call Mary the Mother of God. Catholics are not ashamed of praying to Mary. In fact, Catholicism does not hide her faith or theology from anyone. When Catholics use the rosary beads and the crucifix, they are not ashamed of manifesting their relics. Catholicism taught me not to be ashamed of my faith, and to speak out about Jesus Christ.

I overcame much of the Marian obstacle after the confirmation. I struggled with Mary's ascension into heaven. It was believed that Mary's body was taken into heaven according to traditions of the early

Church. There were no accounts of anyone preserving Mary's body or bones. If there were bones or a body, she would have been preserved in a shrine like Peter.[19] Interesting, but who truly knows? How did I know if she was taken up in heaven or not? I had a major question about Mary's impeccability. I agree with her immaculate nature. She had to be pure and immaculate to conceive the Son of God. It does make sense to say that a perfect divine can be born of a woman who was innocent. A sinless man being born of a sinner does not make sense. I struggled with the fact that Mary was incapable of sinning. The Scriptures never recorded Mary being tempted. Eve was created perfect, yet she was deceived and disobeyed God willfully. Mary was not divine but human. Eve was human, yet sinned while being in a perfect state.

There is no doubt that Mary was chosen to be the mother of our Lord, God (Jesus Christ). No one else could have taken on the role. I was told by the priests that she did not have a choice. How could Mary say no? The angel just confirmed to her that she was chosen by God. Elizabeth did not say no, but she was chosen to bear a child at an old age. Therefore, Elizabeth did not choose to conceive John the Baptist at an old age. It was God's decree. I can take Calvinists' approach. Rather than saying that Mary chose to bear God's Son, it can be said that God chose Mary to bear His Son. It was not that Mary and the other virgins were chess pawns because God could have chosen any woman at that moment. No other woman could have been given the honor to conceive the Son of God. It was foretold that Mary would be the one that salvation would come through.

The priest at the Steubenville Bible Conference told me that Mary consented to it because she was without sin and it was impossible for her to refuse. God never asked Mary to bear His Son. Gabriel confirmed

---

19 Longenecker, 216

the plan of God to Mary regarding the Savior to come into the world. True, Mary did consent. Mary's consent, I believe, really meant that she acknowledged what happened to her once the Angel Gabriel was revealed to her that she was to conceive the Savior of the world. Reject means that Mary could have denied or not accepted the truth that she was with child. Once Mary was pregnant, she could not take it back or abort the unborn Child. Why would she do that? If Mary was given the freedom to say no, then God must have made the invitation so irresistible that Mary could not say no. Whatever God decrees, it cannot be altered or returned to Him void. Mary was chosen according to the sovereignty of God.

Catholicism believes that Mary had the freedom to choose because she was human. Positions that are of special honor, such as an apostle or prophet, are usually not of choice, in the sense of saying, I desire to be an apostle or a prophet. Every prophet in the Old Testament, like Moses and Jeremiah, said no. None of the prophets resisted it by freewill because they could not turn away from the truth, once confronted with, like Paul. Clearly the Protestants view is that Mary chose, according to her own freewill to obey the voice of the Angel Gabriel. Obviously it seems that it was really not of her own freewill to accept or to decline the call because she was already with child, but she did not know until the Angel Gabriel revealed it to her. However, she did freely accept the word. The Holy Spirit came upon her when she received the good news (Luke 1:35). Therefore, Mary was obedient to the voice of the angel. There are some things we cannot analyze or figure out through human reasoning. So I took teaching on faith. So I left it alone for a while. As I left it alone and came back the doctrine, I gained more insight on Mary's life and ministry (See the Rosary).

Chapter Six
The Seat of Saint Peter

Let me say that the Pope is not the savior or the one that grants salvation. The Pope does not replace Jesus Christ. The Pope is not a god like Caesar was a god of Rome. The papacy has received a bad reputation throughout Church history. The RCIA priest became defensive when I challenged the history of the Roman Catholic Church. I never meant to put the priest on the spot or to attack the Church. I just wanted the Catholic priest to be truthful. The RCIA priest did say that the Church has had its ups and downs, and there has been corruption in the Church. The Church realizes it and has been working on to improve it. The Catholic Church has never claimed to be a perfect Church, The pope was never a dictator. The Catholic Church does not consider the Petrine Ministry to be an "absolute monarchy." There were appropriate limits on papal action. Peter and the apostles were given stewardship over God's household. Peter was the visible head of the Church.[20] The Pope served as a universal pastor. His office was to bind the Church on matters of faith and morals. Peter was the rock of Church. Peter as the rock did not imply Peter's description (not taking the place of Jesus as the founder of the Church), but his calling (it was his role as leader over Christ's Church.[21] Jesus was the Chief Cornerstone that held the other

---

20 Robert Stackpole. <u>Saint Peter Lives in Rome</u>. (Stockbridge, MA: Marian Press, 2006).96
21 Ibid., 33

stones together. Without the Chief Cornerstone, the Church cannot stand as an administration. He and the Apostles were the foundational stones (Ephesians 2:10). Peter was given keys as Christ's deputy on earth. He has access to whatever belongs to Christ that was given to him by the Heavenly Father. Peter could never accomplish the apostolic mission without the other apostles who shared in the apostleship.[22]

The Vatican II Lumen Gentium stated: "But the college of bishops has no authority, unless it is understood together with the Roman Pontiff, the successors of Peter as its head. The Pope's primacy is over all, both pastors and the faithful."[23]

Did Peter ever make himself pope, or claimed to be pope? The Church taught that the line of the Petrine Ministry came through the successors, the bishops. It was the bishops that carried on the tradition of the apostles.[24] The apostles entrusted the bishops with the task of taking care of Christ's flock. Jesus was the True Shepherd (John 10:1-17). Jesus has been give true ownership over his flock by his Father. True. Jesus did entrust Peter by asking him three time ihe loved him? Jesus told him to "Feed my lambs," "Tend my sheep," and "Feed my sheep" (John 21:15-19, NKJV). The Papacy was controversial throughout the Roman Church Era. I remembered doing a paper on the Great Schism (The two popes, France, and Rome) called "The Avignon Papacy." There were attempts to subject the Pope, Since the pope could not be subjected, groups formed in secret to avoid persecution. There Reformers had problems with the authority of the pope which is called the "Conciliar Movement." Conciliar Movement was a reformed movement in the 14th 15th and 16th century movements that the Catholic Church held

---

22 Ibid. 115, 116
23 Pope John Paul IV. Vatican II. <u>Dogmatic Constitution of the Church, Lumen Gentium.</u> Nov. 21, 1964
24 Ibid., Para. 22, 24, 26

that the supreme authority resided an ecumenical council apart from the papacy. The attempt to subject the papacy was unsuccessful. There was opposition to the conciliar movement from the Roman Catholic Church. The Roman Catholic Church held to the popes as Apostle Peter's successors. The popes were given authority over both temporal and spiritual affairs. The popes were to answer only to God. Failure to subject the popes resulted in the Great Schism.[25]

My Church History studies at Protestant institutions taught that Bishop Leo the Great appointed himself as Pope. Jesus made Peter the Chief Apostle. Jesus said: "Upon this rock, I will build my Church! And gates hell shall not prevail against it" (Matthew 16:18). Almost all the Christian groups believe that Peter was the leader of the apostles. However, the non-Catholic groups do not believe in the papacy or Peter as the first pope. Many groups do believe that the bishops were the successors of the Apostles. This is called the apostolic succession. I was taught and told by Evangelical leaders and members that we were to call "no man father." If this is the case, then why do we call our natural fathers father? True, Jesus always referred to his Heavenly Father. Paul referred to Timothy as his son in the faith. Paul served as a spiritual father to Timothy and Titus.

The word Pope in Latin is papas or spiritual father (Vicar) over Christ's Church. Dispensational theology was very convincing. I am not saying that dispensational theology was wrong about the rapture, tribulation period, and the millennial reign. I have heard many teachings on the Roman Catholic Church's risings from the ashes, or the little horn was to rise up. I knew, for certain, that some Reform groups do not teach dispensational theology. I read a little on Saint Malachy's prophecies on the 112 popes from his time until the tribulation. A dark pope was to

---

25 The Free Dictionary by Farlex website

lead the Church into the Great Tribulation, and the Catholic Church will to be destroyed.[26]

I have heard end times teachers mention some of his works and the Roman Empire in the end times. This was why I was mostly afraid to convert to Catholicism. I knew that there was a lot of animosity between the Protestants and the Catholics during the Reformation. I watched Christian networks' end-time teachers speak about the Anti-Christ. Some view Rome as the city that Daniel prophesied as sitting on the seven hills (Daniel 7). The Pope was the false prophet of the beast (Anti-Christ) (Revelation 13). I was taught in the Reformed circles that the Pope was the anti-Christ. It was Martin Luther, the German Reformer who called the Pope the Anti-Christ by attacking his crown and authority. I seriously doubted that the all popes were evil. There were some greedy and corrupt popes. There has been corruption in the papacy. No, the Pope was never God, or a god, but the Vicar on earth. The Popes have been viewed as false messiahs. The Popes never claimed to have been messiahs. It is true that the Catholics believe that the seat of the Pope is infallible. The pope is not infallible in the moral sense. The word infallible means authoritative. True, the Church was seen as infallible because she believed to be the ground and the pillar of truth (2 Timothy 2:14). Christ empowered his apostles through the Holy Spirit to establish a tradition. The apostles wrote to the churches to carry on the tradition (handling down) of their teachings on Christ. Catholics do not question the authority of the Pope, but some do question some of the decisions on certain issues. At first, I questioned the office of the Pope and the term infallible. In Protestant circles, the word infallible pertains to the word of God alone.

---

[26] www.theworkofGod.org. (Saint Malachy's Prophecies, Popes, and the End of the World)

The Pope is called Holy Father. Some Protestant and Evangelical groups think that Catholicism is a cult. A cult is a group that follows a charismatic leader who claims to be a messiah. Joseph Smith, Elijah Muhammad, M. J. Father Divine, Charles Manuel "Sweet Daddy" Grace, David Koresh, and Jim Jones were cult leaders who were false messiahs. The Catholics do not see the Pope as a messiah, but a Chief Shepherd over God's flock. Some non-Catholics are under the impression that Catholics place popes on pedestals. I have engaged in conversations with Catholics about the Pope. It does seem to be so, but it really is not. Kissing the hand of a Bishop or a Pope is not worship, but some Protestants do see this as worship. Some non-Catholic are under the impression that Catholics worship the Pope over Jesus Christ. I once believed that. When I was a Protestant, I thought, like some Protestants, that Catholics worshipped the Pope. Salvation was through the Pope, I thought. Later, I found it not to be true. Salvation is through the Church, which is Catholic doctrine. The Church is pillar and ground of truth. One cannot judge Catholicism based on a Catholic, but on its theology and tenets. Catholic theology and doctrine from the soul and core was always Biblical and Christ-centered. Jesus and the Trinity is the object of worship, definitely neither Mary nor the Church.

I was taught as a non-Catholic that the keys to the kingdom did not refer to the papacy but rather to all Christians to bind anything and loose anything on heaven and earth that attacks the Body of Christ through the Charismatic gifts of the Spirit. To "bind and loose" referred to a king's right-hand man. Jesus was God in the flesh, but as man, He was the Father's right-hand man, who was given authority to not only forgive sins, but to bind and loose what was on heaven and on earth. Like the sheriff was over the station and jurisdiction of a town or county, the deputy was the one who has the keys to lock and unlock. There is a passage in Isaiah that refers to a king giving his right-hand man the keys and access to everything in the palace. The deputy was guardian over all that belonged to the king. Eliakim replaced Shebna as the king's chamberlain and treasurer. Both men occupied this office. After Eliakim, there were successors of the position as pegs that would not hold. The office was given the keys of the house of David (Isaiah 22:19-25). Evangelical scholars and commentators argue that Eliakim was a type of Christ (NKJV Commentary Thomas Nelson Publishers, 1979).

I agreed with the Evangelical view on this passage because the prophecies pertained to Christ, and not Peter. Jesus said that in His Father's house were many mansions (John 14:2). Revelation 3:7 says, 'These things says He who is holy, He who is true, 'He has the key of David, He who opens and no one shuts, and shuts and no one opens.' He was given the keys to all the mansions and the Father's house." Both parties can call me wishy washy. I could not deny the valid arguments on both sides. The Protestants have a case on this aspect. However, this does not negate the Catholic argument for the office of Peter. Since the Son of Man has been glorified through the resurrection from the Father, he has granted power to his Apostles, especially Peter. Peter was the forefront speaker in Acts 2. Peter was clearly defined as the leader of the Apostles. Peter was the Chief Deputy over Christ's Church on earth, and the other apostles assisted him. All were given keys by Jesus Himself, but Peter was the main keeper of the administrative body on earth, which Catholics call the Vicar. The twelve Apostles, along with Paul and Barnabas respected Peter as the Head. Both Barnabas and Paul ministered together. Paul was not one of the original twelve; he came after Christ's ascension (Acts 9). Barnabas was named an Apostle later (Acts 14:14). Barnabas and Paul did missionary journeys together, and both Apostles separated later (Acts 14:14, 15: 36-41).

Here is the ultimate question. Who are the Popes between Apostle Peter and Leo the Great? So far I have not seen any written documents of the early Church Fathers on the papal office. The early Church Fathers did argue for the office of the Bishop. The Bishops succeeded the Apostles. The Apostles empowered the bishops over certain cities and regions, but there was nothing mentioned about a universal papacy. Perhaps a Catholic apologist or priest could elaborate far better than I could. I am not a Catholic apologist that could cast a verdict on the matter.

The bishop was the living center of the Christian tradition. The presbyters were local bishops. The bishop was a prophetic person, as well as a sacramental person.[27] Polycarp was the one of the first and oldest bishops who sat under the Apostle John. Clement's first letter explained how the apostolic line continued through the presbyters-bishops. The presbyters were the priests to the bishops. This was an order set up by the Apostles. Clement also wrote that the Apostles knew that there would be strife over the office of the bishop.[28] There was an apostolic chain of command long before Leo the Great. Still, there is no mention of the succession for the seat of Peter. A Protestant pointed this out because I was a Protestant who was taught there was no papal office or succession. The Church was entirely too large over the first three centuries, so there had to be order to regulate the divisions and chaos with the body of Christ. There really ought not to have been an argument over the seat of Peter, since the ministry and office of the Apostles did continue on through apostolic succession.

Some non-Catholic sects do agree with the apostolic succession of office. There were some denominations that taught that the Apostles did not pass on the office. I was told by some of my Fundamentalist friends that the Apostles never passed on the charismatic gifts after they died. There were several more groups that believe the same way. However,

---

27 Cyril R. Richardson. <u>Early Church Fathers</u>. (New York: Collier Books; Macmillan Publishing Company, 1st Edition 1970), 20-21
28 Ibid. 39, 63 (Letter of Clement 44:1,2)

some of the same denominations believe in the governing offices of the Church (bishop, elder and deacon). On the other side of the fence were the groups, especially within the Charismatic circles, that believe in the five-fold office. I have sat under some self-proclaimed apostles and prophets who taught that churches were to have the coverings of the apostles and prophets (Ephesians 4:11). Now there are some newly formed groups that are setting up apostolic orders in them, yet these groups reject the idea of a pope. If Peter was an Apostle, then the popes were the Apostles as well.

Peter was called Kephas (the Rock) in Aramaic. The Rock is a person fulfilling a communal role, not just a confession of faith.[29] The Apostle Peter did not merit the office. The Holy Spirit revealed to Peter that Jesus was the Son of God and the Christ. The Spirit revealed this revelation to Peter because Peter was God's choice to be the Chief Apostle to the apostles, not a dictator, but rather one who strengthens and maintains order over the administration. Jesus did not only create in himself a spiritual body; he, also, created a visible infrastructure body to govern his flock. When I was reading through Protestant lenses, I viewed 1 Peter 2:4-10 from an anti-Catholic perspective. I viewed that Peter never claimed to be the foundation. Instead Peter spoke of Jesus as the Chief Cornerstone which the builders rejected. I began to see through Catholic lenses that Peter was speaking of the spiritual body, not the administrative body in this text. It did not make sense to say that the Church sat upon a little rock, while the little rock sat upon a big rock in reference to the letter of Peter. The Church was built upon the foundation of apostles, and prophets are the administration order of the Church which is totally separate from the spiritual body of Christ because Christ is the Head of the spiritual Church (2 Corinthians 12:28, Ephesians 2:20).

---

29 Edmund Hunt. The Fathers of the Church. Pope St. Leo the Great, A New Translation Volume 34. (New York: Fathers of the Church INC., 1957). 109

The New Testament does prove that Peter was the main leader of the Church on earth. Peter was the main spokesperson and main ambassador. Everyone looked to Peter's leadership. I am convinced that Peter held a very special and the most important office among the apostles. Therefore, the office of Peter has to be highly respected.

Chapter Seven
Catholicism is Christianity

AGAIN, IS CATHOLICISM THE TRUE Christian Faith? She, the Mother Church, claims to have been the continuation pillar of the apostles' teachings and order. In fact, Catholicism claims to have been around long before the religious establishment through the apostles maintaining both Jewish and Roman customs. It was believed by many non-Catholics that Christianity existed before Roman Catholicism. Actually Christianity derived from Judaism. It seems that the Roman Catholic Church did not adhere to the Jewish customs that were to be handed down, according to the New Covenant. Many Christian groups did not consider Catholicism to be Christianity because of its Roman-centric traditions. Catholicism was accused of deviating from the actual teachings of the apostles by adding man-made and pagan ideologies. I admit that I had a problem with religious authority because of the feudal political control over people. Feudalism was a social order of classism during the medieval era. Organized religion has suppressed and oppressed its flock. Like the Prophet Ezekiel wrote, "the shepherds of Israel neglected their sheep, fleeced their sheep, and caused the sheep to wander in the wilderness among wolves." The Reformers challenged the corruption in the Roman Catholic Church. Politics and legalism in Christianity have watered down the faith and have caused the faith to be perceived as a gutter-faith filled with hypocrites. Christianity was a name given to the persecuted believers by the Roman Empire.

The Roman Catholic Church and the Protestant sects were reprehensible (blamable, guilty) for exploitation, colonialism, and putting to death Christian martyrs for heresy. True, there were radical Christian groups and Christians that opposed organized religion. When people think of religion, people think of Christian denominations. There were so-called non-denominational Christians that believed that the religion was man-made. Unfortunately, religion has been given a bad name over the ages. Organized religion is seen and viewed by many as having political control over its followers.

There was a whole lot of truth in this. It has been proven historically. Human civil government was created by God and even spiritual government. In spite of corrupted human authority, there could be no anarchy (overthrowing objective authority), or there would be social and moral chaos (Romans 13). There had to Moral Objective Order in order to regulate the people, or there would have been chaos. Radical groups always reacted to religious organizations that were morally and spiritually corrupted.

Some non-Catholics believe that the Roman Catholic Church began with Constantine, who legalized Christianity as the official religion of the Roman Empire. Christianity was no longer Christianity since the faith was legalized. Christianity was no longer the minority in the Roman Empire. The Church gained status quo once the religious persecution ceased against her. Cathedrals were being built. The Church was the tallest building in Europe in medieval times. The Church was seen as the beacon of hope.

I learned in seminary that if a person was alive during the ancient Roman Catholic era, he or she had to be part of the Church. If a person did not have Rome as his or her mother, then he or she did not have God as his or her Father. Catechism of the Catholic Church teaches that there is no salvation outside the Church. A non-Catholic would see this as the Church being exalted over God and Jesus Christ, which would have been considered as idolatry. Catholicism believed that she has preserved the line of the apostolic teachings of the Apostles. Scripture was subject to tradition. The Bible was the Magisterium (Rule of Faith). Catholicism was accused of adding and taking away Scripture. There was a tradition that was handed down by the apostles, but it was believed to have been up to the Church to interpret the Didache (Apostles' teachings). The Church was believed to have been Infallible. The Catholic Church had no objection to asking questions about the beliefs of the Church's teachings, but one was not to question objectively, in the sense of attacking her teachings. Denominations were the same way, and even cults did not like for you to question their doctrines with an objective approach like the Reformers did. I came into the faith with many questions, but the priest gave me a funny look because I knew the Scriptures, unlike the rest of the candidates.

Some Christians believe that that the Catholic traditions are pagan. There was nowhere in Scripture about celebrating the feast of saints, declaring a dead saint a saint, or celebrating a day of veneration for Mary or the saints. Catholicism admitted that these practices were not Biblical but based on what was passed down traditionally through the Apostolic Fathers. Some non-Catholics called this extra-Biblical.

I was taught, as a Protestant, that the Roman Catholic Church was the whore of Satan and the advocate of the Anti-Christ. My first impression of the Catholic Church was the relics. Catholicism was filled with relics. I have been taught by some Evangelical groups that Catholicism is a pagan religion through Emperor Constantine. If Catholicism is a pagan religion, then Protestantism is also pagan because she is the daughter of Catholicism. In fact, many of the holidays that both Protestants and Catholics celebrate derived from paganism, especially Christmas and Easter. Constantine changed the pagan holidays into the Christian holidays. I learned this through the Jehovah's Witnesses discipleship. I do not really blame the Jehovah's Witnesses and the Unitarians and other groups for not practicing such customs.

Truthfully, I am not that fond of the holidays that have derived from pagan origins. Tertullian said that God prohibited idols to be worshipped. Tertullian grieved that the faithful were bringing pagan idols into the Church after coming from the adversary's workshop. Idol-artificers were chosen into the ecclesiastical order. In fact, Tertullian opposed celebrating pagan holidays in the Church.[30] The Roman Catholic Church fought very hard to keep out paganism. There was anti-Semitism in the empire. I have had Messianic Jews tell me and show me that Emperor Constantine wanted to do away with anything thing that was Jewish through a document a few years ago. I had a Jewish apostle show me through Scripture that we were to celebrate the Jewish Feasts, according to the New Testament. The apostle was anti-Christian. The apostle told me that the Catholic Church did away with the Jewish customs and embraced pagan traditions by incorporating them into the Church. These became known as the Christian feasts. The Churches, as a whole, including Catholicism, acknowledge that Christianity derived from Judaism.

I admitted that Roman Catholicism used a lot of Platonic and Aristotelian concepts to formulate many doctrines of the Church. Catholicism used Greek philosophy to interpret theology. There were many things that Catholicism incorporated into the political religion of the Roman Empire. Protestants hold Socrates, Plato, and Aristotle to in high-esteem, especially Socrates. All three were Greek Pagans, not Christians. Their philosophies were widely used in churches. Therefore, this still does not make Christianity a pagan faith. Romanism was added

---

30 <u>The Ante-Nicene Fathers A.D. 325, Volume III</u>. 1976. (Tertullian Works" De Idolatria," On Idolatry), Ch. VII, XIII.62,64, 69

to Christianity, which caused sects to become opposed to the Roman Catholic Church. There were things that the Protestant Reformers wanted to purge the Church of, such as relics. Protestant movements and Evangelical movements tried to bring radical changes and return to the Apostles' teachings that the Catholic believed to have deviated from. The Protestant movement caused several schisms within a 500-year span. If Catholicism is not a true faith, Protestantism is not either because she is of the same bloodline as Roman Catholicism, although Protestants do not claim her mother. Technically, we all need to go back to Judaism since our spiritual identity derived from her.

I speak from years of religion experiences. Each sect claimed to have been the true faith. I have had Church of Christ co-workers argue with me that Jesus established his Church in 33 ½ A.D. The only appropriate title was the Church of Christ, not denominational names because these names were not Biblical. I remembered when the Jehovah's Witnesses came to my house many times for Bible study. The Witnesses would always ask, "If Jehovah established an organization on earth, which organization would that be?" I always said "none" because Christ established a spiritual church. I knew that the Jehovah's Witnesses wanted me to reply with the answer the Watchtower. The sects that were called Apostolic Churches insisted that I join their Church because it was not Trinitarian and was baptized in the name of Jesus alone according to Acts 2:32(one person), not the Trinity (three persons). Some groups say that what Jesus spoke about in Matthew 28 were just titles, not persons.

I agree that there had to have been a visible Church. The visible church was the order. There had to be order to prevent chaos. I was taught as a Reform seminarian that there were two types of Churches: the visible Church consists of both true and professing Christians and the invisible Church is the true elect whom God has chosen before the foundation of the world. Catholicism teaches that the visible Church is

Christ's visible administration on earth based on order and structure. The Spiritual Church was the universal Church that consisted of Christians all over. The Spiritual Church was the covenantal relationship between Christ and His body. Catholicism is the most orderly faith that I have ever seen, yet she remains strong and effective.

Chapter Eight
Trinitarian Godhead

THE MOST CONTROVERSIAL THEOLOGICAL TOPIC was always the humanity and divinity of Christ along with the doctrine of the Trinity. The Church always taught that Jesus was fully human and divine. Jesus was the Incarnated Word of God (John 1:14). Here was the irony when it comes to Catholicism as a cult to many non-Catholics. The Trinity derived from the Catholic Church. Catholicism was accused of Quadrity (Four Gods). Quadrity is contrary to Catholic and apostolic teaching. Mary was not divine in any way or on par with the Father, the Son, and the Holy Spirit. The Trinity was the doctrine of the Church. It was in the beginning, and the doctrine remains part of Catholic tradition. Latria is Latin for adoration and worship which is to the divine Trinity.

Gregory of Nazianz said: "For us there is one God, because the Godhead is One; and though we believe in Three, we refer to One whatever has its source in Him .... Neither are they separated in will, nor divided in power, nor are any of the qualities of divisible things to be found here ... and there is one mingling of light, as if in three suns joined to each other."[31]

Monotheism was the belief in a single deity such as God. Deuteronomy 6:4 states that God is One. Both Christianity and Judaism believed in

---

31 William A. Jergens. <u>The Faith of the Early Fathers Volume 2</u>. (Collegeville, MN: The Liturgical Press, 1979),33. The works of Gregory of Nazianz Paragraph 997, verse 31, 14.

the one true God, the God of Abraham, Isaac, and Jacob. Islam believed in one God, Allah, the God of Abraham and Ishmael. Cults have often accused the traditional sects that teach the doctrine of the Trinity. In the human mind, three persons equal one God, but this does not make sense, especially Jesus as the Son of God and God in the flesh.

Tritheism is the belief that the Godhead consists of three persons, three gods with equal power and substance. This is contrary to the Christian doctrine of the Trinity. The question is: Was the Trinity a Jewish concept or a Gentile concept? Jews rejected the deity of Christ Jesus as God-man. The Jewish belief was that God remains in eternity. So intermediaries acted as God by speaking with authority, according to a couple of Jewish teachers I met and debated with. God becoming flesh was considered blasphemy. Some anti-Trinitarian groups believe that the Trinitarian doctrine was formulated by Emperor Constantine himself through the council of Nicene. If Catholicism is a cult, then why did all the Trinitarian denominations embrace the Trinity since it is the belief in one God? It does not make sense. Mary was never of the Trinity. This is absurd.

The best ways I learned to understand the Trinity were both ontological and economical. Economical Trinity derives from the Greek word Oikonomia which means household management. It involved roles and jobs and positions in the household. Ontological Trinity focuses on who God is. Ontology is the philosophical belief of being and nature. The philosophy involved both properties and attributes.

In seminary, I had a theology professor had us to do papers on Systematic Theology, and one the papers was on the Trinity. I wrote that each person in the Godhead had three different roles yet were equal in substance and in power. The professor's feedback was that I had been careful not to go into the ontological argument without damaging the doctrine of the Trinity. It was hard to avoid the teaching on subordinate

Trinity. The Son and the Holy Spirit voluntarily became agents of the Father, yet both the Son and the Holy Spirit are eternal, not created.

The Son co-existed with the Father as the Logos (John 1:1). The Holy Spirit co-existed as the Spirit of God (Genesis 1:2). Jesus and the Father are one, both ontologically and economically (John 10:30). Jesus's claims to have been from heaven caused controversy among the Jews. The Gentiles, especially the Greeks, were very philosophical. When the Greeks became Christians, the Greek ways were not altered. The Greeks distinguished between spirit and matter.[32] The Church Fathers, mostly Greeks, debated and attempted to dissect the nature of the Godhead by explaining not only the nature and essence, but mainly divine substance.

"The Most Holy Trinity is the central mystery of our Christian faith and life, the source of all other mysteries of our faith …. In brief, the doctrine of the Trinity teaches that Jesus is the visible image of God. The Holy Spirit is sent by the Father in the name of the Son."[33] Catholicism is monotheistic. Definitely, the faith is Trinitarian. Like the Jehovah's Witnesses, non-Trinitarian groups argued that the Trinity derived from paganism because the Trinity confirms "three distinct persons, one God, one in essence and in substance." For years, I questioned the Trinity. There were some who attacked the Divinity and Humanity of Christ like The DaVinci Code that claims to be fiction. The DaVinci Code writings argued that both Jesus's Divinity and "the Son of God" were officially voted in at the Council of Nicea under Emperor Constantine in 325 A.D.

The Church doctrine was already in the making and taught by some before 325. Catholicism says that the doctrine of the Trinity was

---

32 Harry R. Boer. <u>A Short History of the Early Church</u>. (Grand Rapids, Mi: W.B. Eerdman's Publishing Company, 1976). 108
33 Michael Pennock. <u>This is Our Faith, A Catholic Catechism for Adults</u>. (Norte Dame, IN: Ave Maria Press, 1998). 34 The author's source if from CCC 232-237

already taught in the early Church. Arius was the one who raised the question and opposed Jesus being God and pre-existent.[34] on YouTube, many times, I watched theologians and religious cults argue that Jesus was Serapis Christus, a Greek-Egyptian god born under Emperor Constantine's reign as God, 325 AD. Jesus's image was believed to have derived from Ptolemy, later named Meryamun Setepenre. Amun, which means "God, Chosen by Ra (God)," became the first European Pharaoh of Egypt as the soter (savior). I heard Ray Hagins's message "The Council that Created Jesus Christ" on YouTube. Arius was of African descent and he opposed the deity of Christ, formerly Serapis.[35]

I would not have been surprised if these claims were historically true. There was some truth to the rumor that the Roman Church hid many truths from the people to cover up its certain acts. There was a lot of truth in this. Jesus's images are in black and white or Spanish. James Cone's Theology of Black Liberation believed that God was black because he was on the side of the oppressed, and that the white Jesus was Eurocentric.[36] We must be careful not to confine Jesus to our own culture because God is far greater than any matrix or box. I was told by black cult groups that God was black, and the white Jesus was really Satan. I was challenged by certain Muslims, especially black Muslims in the barbershops and the prison ministry that we worship three Gods (tritheism). Most denominations do agree on the doctrine of the Trinity, yet many non-Catholic groups do not believe that Catholics are Christians. The Trinity was long resolved for me years ago. For years,

---

34 Mark Shea. The DaVinci Deception. (West Chester, PA: Ascension Press, 2006).67

35 Ray Hagins. You-Tube. WWW.Hit on the head.com, Historical Evidences that Proves "Jesus Christ Never Existed and was Created by Emperor Constantine", April 25, 2013

36 James H. Cone. God of the Oppressed. (New York: Seabury Press, 1975). 14,35

I questioned the Trinity, since my discipleship under the Jehovah's Witnesses. The Jehovah's Witnesses were very convincing and studious in their arguments against the Trinity. Christianity can be complicated at times, especially on this doctrine. How can Jesus be God and the Son of God at the same time? If was Jesus was God, where was God for three days, and how can God die if He was immortal? Since God could not be tempted, how was Jesus God? Was Jesus praying to Himself? Praxeus, the Father of Modalism, along with his protégé Sabballeus taught one God singular. There are some Jesus Only Faiths that teach Modalism (God in three masks in three dispensations, but not three separate persons). Modalism spirit exists today in some Churches who see the Father, the Son, and the Holy Spirit as only three titles rather than persons.

For the first three centuries, the humanity and divinity of Christ was debated and unresolved until the Council at Nicene in 381 A.D. Constantine saw that the Church was divided and appointed a council to maintain order. Most Protestants agreed with the doctrine of the Trinity, which was derived from Catholicism because it was Catholicism that formulated the doctrine based upon Scripture. The Scriptures were needed to formulate the doctrine. If Catholicism was not a Christian faith, then why not question the Trinity as well? I was taught that one could not explain the Trinity, to just accept it by faith. If the doctrine was formulated by man, then it can be explained. The early fathers Tertullian, Athanasius, and Augustine explained it well. If the veneration of Mary was questioned by denominations, then Jesus's divinity ought to have been questioned such as the (God-Man) God by nature, but ministered as man. A non-Trinitarian would use this as an argument that mainstream Christianity worshiped Jesus as a god since He was believed to have been a mere man, which was a heresy in the early Church. John of Damascus argued that, if Jesus was a mere man, then it would have been considered idolatry.

In the Old Testament, God was no doubt monotheistic. The Shema says that God is One and the only true God (Deuteronomy 6:4). The Word did not yet become flesh at that time. After the Word became flesh, then God was expressed through the Son (John 1:1, 14). So now we have a God-man image to worship. God is worshipped in the body of Christ where the whole fullness of the Godhead resides.[37] Irenaeus argued that God was incomprehensive, so we were not to attempt to question or to attack the Godhead, the substance we cannot truly explain until we see Him face to face. Jesus revealed the nature of the Father, virtually, economically, and His communion with the Father (John 14:9).

The Trinity was considered as being incomprehensible, but the Son revealed the fellowship and economy of the Trinity. Jesus revealed His oneness with the father (John 10:30; 14). The Son was the central focus and argument in the early Church because Jesus claimed to be divine. The Trinitarian controversy was heated among theologian, especially Arius vs. Athanasius. The debate was ongoing for a long period of time. During the Mass, Catholics recite the Athanasian Creed (Nicene-Constantinople Creed). The creed states: "Consubstantial with the Father, Light from Light, True God from True God, begotten not made, one in Being with the Father." Before Abraham was, I am (John 8:58). Identity precludes plurality.[38] Athanasius argued that Jesus was consubstantial with the Father. According to Athanasius, a creature cannot redeem another creature. Jesus definitely did not sacrifice Himself as God, but as man because the Immortal God could not die.

As a former disciple of the Jehovah's Witnesses, I was taught that Jesus and Adam were equivalent because man was the offender and not God.

---

37 William A. Jurgens. <u>The Faith of the Early Fathers Volume 3</u>. (Collegeville, MD: The Liturgical Press, 1979). 337. Works of St. John Damascene Article Paragraph 2363

38 John Paul II. <u>A Catechesis on the Creed. God Father and Creator, Volume One</u>.(Boston, MA: Pauline Books & Media, 1996).170

According to the Watchtower's teaching, Jesus was Michael the Archangel. Jesus was pre-existent as God's first creation, and He co-created with God the Father the universe. Mankind and angels are not equivalent. There was and is not retribution for the fallen angels. Arius believed that there was a time that Jesus was not (pre-existent). Arius went down in history as a heretic. It did not mean that Arius was an evil man or Christian. Proverbs chapters 3 and 8 reveal wisdom brought forth by God, who was along His side. The Son could not exist without the Father. Jesus spoke as the Word; Jesus spoke from the Torah. Some of the early apologists taught that Jesus was the highest creature and that the Son was subordinate to the Father because God cannot concern himself with matter. This is called subordinationism.[39] Tertullian gave a great illustration of the Trinity. In fact, Tertullian was one of the first to explain the Trinity. The rays could exist without the sun. God could never procreate. God could never procreate a Son because He was and is Spirit. God did not procreate angels but created them as sons of God. Adam was not procreated, but created by God out of the dust. Adam was the son of God, but Jesus was the begotten Son of God through conception by the Holy Spirit. Jesus's true identity was the Logos, the Breathing Torah that created the universe (John1:14). Jesus was the wisdom of God (1 Corinthians 1:30).

When I was in a Calvinist seminary, I was taught that the Trinity operated throughout human history. The Father was in the Old Testament, the Son in the New Testament from birth to his death to his resurrection and ascension, and the Holy Spirit appeared during Pentecost. The Holy Spirit is the minister in this dispensational age.

Pope John Paul's message to the general audience stated: "The Spirit of God not only reveals the meaning of history, but instills the strength to cooperate with the divine plan that is fulfilled in it. In the light of the

---

39 Harry Boer, 110

Father, the Son, and the Spirit, history ceases to be a succession of events that fade into the abyss of death, but becomes a land made fruitful by the seed of eternity, a path leading to that sublime goal in which ..."[40] "God will be in it all (I Cor. 15:28)."[41] God exists outside of space and time and can intervene at will. God is both transcendent and immanent.

Since Catholicism formulated the doctrine of the Trinity, Catholicism went much deeper into explaining the doctrine of the Trinity. The Trinity was not only One Divine Substance and Essence and Nature, it was also Economical. Jesus reveals the economy of the Godhead. "I and my Father are one" (John 10:30). The Godhead works as one, the Son and the Holy Spirit are the expressions of the Godhead. In conclusion, most Christian parties agree that the Trinity played its role in salvation. When we behold Him face to face, then our questions will be answered and the curiosity will cease (1 Corinthians 13).

---

[40] Pope John Paul II. <u>Dogmatic Poems, XXI, Hummus Alias</u>: 37, 510-511. February 9, 2009

[41] John Paul II. <u>The Trinity's Embrace God's Saving Plan, Volume Six</u>. (Boston, MA: Pauline Books, 2002).317

Chapter Nine
The Mass: Christ's Presence

THE MASS WAS MY BIGGEST obstacle during my RCIA experience. The doctrine of Transubstantiation brought many questions to my mind. My parish priest told us upfront that, if one still thought that the Mass was a vain and pagan ritual, we should not take the final step on Saturday night, Easter Vigil, and Confirmation. I asked the Holy Spirit to help me understand this practice. I knew the time of Confirmation was approaching. I had learned to embrace the doctrine according to faith, not reason. There were philosophical objections to the Eucharist. Many non-Catholics saw the Catholic view as being contrary to Scripture. I did not understand the miracle being done scientifically. Some things we just have to let alone, rather than try to figure them out through reasoning, which makes things more complicated. John Salza said: "Now for the Catholic rejoinder: The mystery of the Eucharist is not contrary to reason; it is above reason. That is because it is a miracle, and the Catholic understanding of the miracle is backed by the very words of Jesus and twenty centuries of Catholic tradition.... The Eucharist is a doctrine that transcends our limited human capacity to fully understand."[42]

The Reformed view opposed the notion of Transubstantiation. I was taught as a former Reformed student that the elements did not change in themselves. I was taught by Evangelical professors that the priest offered the

---

[42] John F. Salza. The Biblical Basis for the Eucharist. (Huntington, IN: Our Sunday Visitor Publishing Division, 2008). 159

bones and blood of dead martyrs as Jesus's body and blood. This would have been cannibalism. In seminary, I learned that John Wycliffe, the English Reformer, wrote a book on Transubstantiation which attacked the Catholic Church. Wycliffe argued that the doctrine was instituted through the Fourth Lateran Council in 1300. Jesus saying was symbolic, and not literal. Wycliffe would have been one of the earliest Reformers, definitely before Martin Luther. Wycliffe was believed to be Augustinian, according to what I was taught by Reformed professors. As a Protestant, I was taught that the Lord's Supper was just mere symbol, or an outward sign of an invisible grace. Transubstantiation can be traced back to Justin Martyr and even Irenaeus in the second century. I discovered, in the works of the Early Church Fathers, that the supper was taken literally, especially in the works of Justin Martyr. "We call this food Eucharist … for not as common bread, nor common drink do we receive these, but since Jesus was made incarnate by the word of God and had been made into the Eucharist by the Eucharistic prayer set down by him, and by the change of which our blood and flesh is nourished, is both the flesh and blood of the incarnate Jesus."[43]

Saint Ireneaus confirms the same thing in his writings. He said that the bread from the earth was no longer common bread but the Eucharist. Our bodies were nourished by the bread and wine.[44] The Didache (Apostle's Teachings) said that only the believers in the family of God took part in the Eucharist.[45]

One Sunday in a month or every couple of months, I saw the women in the Church preparing the table for Sunday communion. In the Baptist Church, we used Welch's grape juice and Saltine crackers,

---

[43] William A. Jergens. <u>The Faith of the Fathers Volume 1</u>. (Collegeville, MN: The Liturgical Press, 1970).55
[44] Ibid.,95,99
[45] Ibid.,3

then later wafers. Some denomination used the same thing. When I first visited the Catholic Church, I was shocked to see Catholics use real wine. I unknowingly took a communion without first being confirmed into the faith. Until I fully understood the significance of the Mass, I had to receive spiritual communion by crossing my hands over my chest so that the priest could give me a spiritual blessing. I never understood until after conversion about discerning the Lord's body. In a way, many Catholics have a misunderstanding about Protestant views on the Lord's Supper. I observed that many Protestant churches take the Lord's Supper seriously. Denominations do highly respect communion or sacraments, whichever term each uses. Mere Symbol is a term used loosely. Symbolic and Mere Symbol were totally different from each other. Symbolic was the appropriate term used in denominations. Many sects believed that there was spiritual significance in the Lord's Supper which might have been contrary to the Catholic view, definitely not transubstantiation.

When I was a pre-teen, I asked my mother what the communion meant? My mother said: "If you don't know, don't take it!" Since then I knew communion was a serious matter. I grew up in a church that taught that one's heart must be right with God before taking communion. No believer was to take communion unworthily. To take communion in an unworthy manner brought damnation and even sickness. I always understood that one must examine his heart and make peace with his brother who he had been offended by. This seems to give Catholicism the case for the doctrine of transubstantiation.

True, Jesus did not say, "This is my symbol." Jesus said, "This is my body that was broken for you. This is my blood that was shed for you." Catholicism taught this passage of Scripture as literal. I will say this: we cannot understand such mysteries as this through our human reasoning. I was trying to figure out how the elements could actually change into the literal body and blood of Christ. I knew that the Eucharist was not cannibalism. Cannibalism was forbidden for Israel to practice. Many of Jesus's followers turned away when He said, unless you eat of my body and drink of my blood, you cannot have life. Many thought He was talking about cannibalism. Jesus was speaking of His spiritual body, not His natural body (John 6). His divinity resided in the physical body God had prepared for Him. Jesus was the embodiment of wisdom. Paul wrote that Jesus was the wisdom of God (1 Corinthians 1:30). Solomon wrote that Wisdom gives out her invitation to enter her gates and eat and drink from her. Moses and the Israelites were provided manna (bread) that came down from heaven in the wilderness. Jesus said that He is the Bread of Life (John 6)

In a nutshell, the real meaning of the Mass means "to go forth." In other words, we are to live out the Mass outside the church walls. The Mass was not confined to just the Eucharist (the elements), which was the heart of the Mass because Christ met us and was present in the Mass. "The Spirit invites us into deeper relationship and discipleship with Jesus the Christ. Three primary symbols are the Assembly, the Word, and the Eucharist." Also, "if there is one thing that characterizes Catholics, it is our sense of community. In a culture wrapped in individualism, the Catholic tradition says it's not about 'me,' but about 'we.' Jesus saves us not as a person, but as a people."[46]

Catholicism places its emphasizes on the corporate body rather than just on an individual. Catholics never denied that each person has to give an account to God for his or her own actions. Catholics never denied individual judgment. Catholicism saw itself as both a corporate and spiritual body. The Bible says that we are not to forsake our assembly. The gifts of the Holy Spirit were for the body rather than just the individual. No person is ungifted. One's strengths can be one's weakness. We all

---

[46] Micheal J. Daley. <u>Our Catholic Symbols, A Rich Spiritual Heritage</u>. (New London, CT: Twenty Third 23rd Publications, 2009). 79

have gifts to contribute to the body of Christ. I believed the reason why Catholicism was so successful in its mission was because she thought as a community rather than as an individual. I was taught as a Baptist, an Evangelical, and a Protestant that one was to have a personal relationship with Jesus, yet we are to fellowship and assemble together. There was not really much disagreement between the church groups. My parish priest told me after the confirmation several times that meditation, the mass, and fellowships with the believers were very essential to my spiritual walk. Without these three, I would have become weak and drifted away from the communion with the fellow saints. The Mass was where Christ strengthens us and nurtures us through himself. The Mass was and is not re-sacrificing Christ through blood, because Christ has already made the Ultimate Sacrifice.

Jeff Cavins said: "Every time we go to mass, we should be struck by the fact that God has come to earth, suffered, died, and now asks us to follow in His footsteps. At the end of every mass, we must leave with the attitude: Not only am I going to join myself to Him in His sacrifice, but I am going to live that sacrifice when I exit the door and go to my home, my work, and my neighbors. In short, I'm going to become like Jesus in every area of my life.[47]

I agree with the author and the Catholic view on the Mass. Jesus said, "Let our light so shine that people may see our good works and glorify the Heavenly Father" (Matthew 5:16). I learned as, a former Calvin student, that we participate in the sacraments, not because we are worthy, but we unworthy. Right, we are not perfect people. That is why we need the Eucharist. I do not mean to be harsh, not against the Eucharist itself, but against some Catholic members. Many Catholics, that I observed (not all but enough in number to say), are sensitive to

---

[47] Scott Han & Regis J. Flaherty. Catholics for a Reason III, Scripture and the Mystery of the Mass. (Steubenville, OH: Emmaus Road, 2004).158

the body and blood of Christ during the Mass, but some Catholics leave their spirituality behind the walls. When Church is over, some behave like the world. Some of their noses are so high up, that they are drowning, just like Christians in the denominations put on the world and take off Christ after Church service. This is called "hypocrisy." The Church has been given a bad reputation in the department of hypocrisy. This was according to the lost and the world's point of view. Catholicism never taught that going to the Mass alone gets one into heaven, rather the Mass was heaven when we entered in the sanctuary to partake in the liturgy because Jesus Christ meets us in the Mass. The Mass has to be lived out. A Catholic can have intellectual faith, the kind of faith that James said was insufficient for salvation (James 2:24).[48] Therefore, faith without works is dead. Catholics never taught works alone either, but faith and works.

In conclusion, I later understood the deep meaning of the Eucharist. Paul told the members of the Church of Corinth to examine themselves before taking part in the Eucharist (1 Corinthians 6). When we eat the bread and drink the wine, both actually become the actual body and blood of Christ. The Eucharist provides spiritual healing and strength to deal with our personal sins and temptations. We are obligated to make spiritual sacrifices unto God for our reasonable service (Romans 12:1-2). If we partake with him, then we will suffer with Him(John 6). Although Christ presents his presence before us in every Eucharist, we enter heaven with a sense of divine presence, rather than an actual place, but in His kingdom, we will have the Eucharist before His visible presence (Revelation 4).

---

48 Karl Keating. What Catholics Really Believe. 52 Answers to Common Misconceptions about the Catholic Faith. (San Francisco, CA: Ignatius Press, 1992). 22

There will be no Eucharistic sacrifices in heaven when faith and hope pass away. The graces of the sacrament remain for all eternity, in the perfection of Christ's Mystical Body. There will be no baptism, no anointing, and no charism. The sacrifice of the Lamb will be succeeded by the nuptials of the Lamb.[49] Jesus said, "I will not drink of this fruit of the vine from now on until that day when I drink it new with you in my Father's kingdom" (Matthew 26:29, NKJV). There will, after all, be a Mass in heaven.

I concluded that I learned to comprehend the mystery of the Eucharist through becoming a partaker in it. Every time I went the Mass, I wanted to experience the whole person Jesus Christ. There were a couple of Catholic Churches I went to where only the priest received the whole host, both the body and blood of Christ. I went during the winter time. I asked why the members only received the body of Christ, and not the blood of Christ? When I went, I felt cheated. After, it took over three years to convince me that the bread and wine became the actual body and blood of Christ. I sensed that it was a lack of faith in a sense because it was the flu season, so the blood (wine) was not given. If Jesus becomes the actual Eucharist, then there ought to be power and healing in the Eucharist, in spite of our cold and flu symptoms. This bothered me a whole lot, but it did not change my belief in the transubstantiation once I was convinced of the doctrine. If some of the Catholic Churches thought that way, then why did the Church not put the wine (blood) in little cups like Baptists since there was a slight amount of skepticism?

I watched The Web of Faith 2 on EWTN, when callers send in their comments and questions. One of the priests said that the wafer contains the whole heavenly host, and the priest has to have both the body and

---

49 Abbot Vonier. A Key to the Doctrine of the Eucharist. (USA: Zaccheus Press, 2003).173

blood of Christ since he is offering up the sacrifice to God himself. The lay people could still receive the whole host in the form of bread. So I later understood it. Therefore, it is a matter of faith when taking it. The heart of the mass is God's presence. We do not have to die to go into God's presence. Christ meets us in every Mass service. In conclusion, the Mass is not so much the elements themselves, but the Lamb of God who takes away the sins of the world (John 1:29). This is what the Book of Revelation is all about.

Chapter Ten
The Day of Confirmation

WHAT WAS REALLY GOING ON in the back of my mind? I struggled with the conversion process because I still had many questions about Catholicism. The RCIA was a fast-paced class. At first, I felt pressured to convert over. One cannot take in two thousand years of Church history and doctrine. It took three RCIAs before confirmation. During the third year, I felt a dark cloud hovering over my head. I was afraid to make the move because of the judgments I would receive from my friends who were Evangelical and my family. Most of all, I was afraid of God since I was warned by a woman who prophesied me going into the Jehovah's Witnesses, that God was going bring judgment on me if I did so. So I did not want to experience this again. The spirit of fear was upon me. I knew that God did give us the spirit of fear, but a sound mind. I had fellow-Catholics in the bookstore guiding me through the journey process. A woman who worked in the Catholic bookstore told me to read Weeds among the Wheat which was a book about discernment. The book defined the spirit of discernment. He defined discernment as "one seeking the perfect will of God." Here are three presuppositions of Discernment, according to Thomas A. Green: 1.) A desire to God's will, which also means commitment to faith in the Lord. 2.) Openness to God. We cannot block ourselves from experiencing God if we are to be open to God, and 3.) A knowledge of God. This knowledge is an enlightened faith.[50] The author also defined the nature and purpose. He said: 1.) Discernment presupposes a person who truly desires to accomplish God's work in concrete, confused situations of life; 2.) Discernment further presupposes a person who is truly open to be taught by and led by the Lord, and 3.) Finally, the first two presuppositions must be fruitful because the discerner must know, in the Biblical sense, an experimental knowledge born of love.[51] Paul prayed that God may open the Church of Ephesus's eyes to God's revelation (Ephesians 1). In order to know God intimately, one must have prudent knowledge and understanding of who He is. Until I understood the perfect will of God for my life, I had to take spiritual communion so that God would grace my calling and allow me to endure the spiritual journey. As the Easter Vigil was approaching, the veil of heavy burden of fear was being uplifted. The Catholic journey was really beginning for me after the confirmation.

I was willing to finish the journey through the RCIA. I knew that the enemy did not want me to continue. A Pentecostal woman told me that it was the Holy Spirit warning me. I was not going to let a so-called prophecy stop me from pursuing my divine purpose. I was still holding to my subjective conscience on interpretation of Scripture. I had to agree with Martin Luther when he stood up at the Diet of Worms against the Catholic Council and the emperor. Luther argued that, for one to go against conscience, was neither right nor safe. The theme of my subjective thinking was not to go against the truth of God.[52]

Catholicism places its emphasis on objective truth. Catholicism believes that the Church's job is to inform the conscience. The Church needs objective norm to abide by as a corporate body. I constantly

---

50 Thomas H. Green. <u>Weeds Among the Wheat, Discernment: Where Prayer & Action Meet</u>. (Norte Dame, IN: Ava Maria Press, 1984). 58-61
51 Ibid.,63
52 www.BrainyQuotes.com,2016 Martin Luther Quotes(Website)

questioned the Church's objective truth before and after confirmation. No objective norm is perfect, but we need norm to maintain order. I knew then that God was cultivating me through the Catholic Church. God placed me where He wanted me to be, maybe temporarily or permanently. The priest told the candidates that this may not be the perfect place, but it was best place for us at this time. The best thing for me was for me was to be in the Catholic Church and view it as a training ground. I believed that God was going to use me in both the Protestant and the Catholic Churches to share his word.

When the priest laid hands on me, I felt the Holy Spirit releasing the spirit of heaviness off of me. No, I did not speak in tongues. I was not slain in the Spirit. I felt that I would get a better understanding of the Catholic faith by being on the inside than from the outside. I had the support of Catholic sponsors by my side the whole time.

On the night of the Confirmation, right before I took the final step, I was truly afraid. I felt as if I was joining a cult. I felt, if I entered the faith, then I would have sold my soul to the devil. The moment the priest laid his hands on me, though, the fear left and the veil was lifted. I asked God to be with me through the process. God had a purpose for me to have gone through the process. Whenever I tried to go back, God would turn me around. I knew that I would suffer more rejection from those I knew in the Protestant churches. The moment some of my friends found out I had become Catholic, I sensed my friends beginning to shun me.

Catholics believe that suffering is a virtue, not a vice. There is virtue in suffering. Suffering matures the spirit man and builds spiritual character (Romans 5). All my life I felt rejected because I was different, but I realized that God set me up to endure suffering for His purpose. I remembered the Jehovah's Witnesses showing me the passage in Matthew when Jesus told His disciples to take up their cross and follow Him (Matthew 16:24-26).

I confess that I converted through wounded pretenses. I mean that my hurts from other groups brought me to the doorsteps of the Catholic Church. My mother, who was a retired as pastor told her children to stay under a covering. I was open to enemy attacks and temptations. A sheep was not to wander out on its own without a shepherd. I was taught that sometimes the shepherd had to break the legs of the sheep to keep it from wandering off. God had to break my legs so that I would not wander off. Sheep are gentle, yet gullible animals that can be manipulated. I knew that had God placed me under someone who loves Him and serves Him with humility.

I understood the Confirmation as entering into a spiritual covenant, rather than just an organization. "Our Catholic faith affirms then that confirmation completes and perfects the grace received at Baptism. Baptism gives the Holy Spirit, and incorporates us unto Christ and His Church …. Confirmation fortifies the soul for purgations of the beginner ….Confirmation serves as a seal that completes, and total belonging to Christ."[53]

Thomas Richard also gave three purposes for confirmation:

> Confirmation is the interior purification of the illuminative stage.
>
> Confirmation is for the trials of the dark night of the senses.
>
> Confirmation is for the deep and mystical purifications of the dark night of the spirit.[54]

What did confirmation mean to me, according to my personal experience?

---

53 R. Thomas Richard. <u>The Ordinary Path to Holiness</u>. (Staten Island, NY; the Society of St. Paul, 2003). 169
54 Ibid 169.

During the conversion and journey process, I had to understand the meaning of the sacraments. Sacraments are acts of receiving God's grace. The Medieval term 1150-1200 is from the Latin term sacramentium, which meant an oath, vow, or consecration (www.thefreedictionary.com). God was setting me apart for His purpose. I knew that I was not my own individual, but I was now property of God. Partaking in the Eucharist for the first time meant suffering for the sake of Christ. In other words, I was a partaker in His suffering. I was baptized into his suffering. I saw that my obligation was to God, and there was no turning back. My struggle was internal; there was a tug of war occurring in my soul. My soul was at war with itself. Confirmation meant newness of life in Christ. Confirmation meant dying to self and the old man. I was afraid to leave where I was. I knew that I had to detach from familiarity, so I could enter into a new calling. I was already baptized. Since I was baptized in the name of the Father, the Son, and the Holy Spirit, my baptism was valid. All I needed was confirmation through the priest. I was already baptized into the spiritual covenant family. I acknowledged myself as a Catholic Evangelical. My roots were Baptist and Evangelical, which were still parts of my religious identity. Catholicism became my new extended family.

Understand the ministry of Paul. Paul was a Jew culturally and religiously, but the Gentiles were his extended family because his ministry was to the Gentiles. I am a Protestant to the Protestants and a Catholic to the Catholics. There is no partiality. We must be all to all people. All I did was become part of an extended family. Spiritually we are all equal, but not positions. God intended for me to understand the nature of the olive branch. The Gentiles were engrafted into the tree of Abraham in place of the tribal branches that fell off, such as the Tribe of Dan (Romans 11). Now the journey really began. The way of Christ is hard and narrow, but it leads to eternal life.

Chapter Eleven
Call to Separation

As a young Catholic convert, I learned that the Spiritual journey is a lifelong process. As we are called to embark on the spiritual journey, we are called to fight on the battlefield along with spiritual warfare. As I embarked on the Catholic journey, I knew that I was even more under attack. I knew that there I was under demonic attack. The closer I came to my destiny, the greater the attacks. Those who I thought were my true friends in the faith even shunned me, as if I had leprosy or some incurable disease.

I learned that Satan himself can transform himself into an angel of light (2 Corinthians 11:14). We all are called to separation or detachment. In order for one to walk with Christ, our character and behavior must change (Romans 12:1-2). Separation means dying to oneself and leaving the former things, such as the old life into the newness of life (Colossians 2:12). Imagine what all the Hebrew prophets of the Old Testament did when God called them out of their present occupations into the office of prophet for life. Some had to leave their families to answer the call of God. The disciples had to leave their former lives and occupations to become fisher of men.

When I converted to Catholicism, I ended up going through a separation process. I did not choose to disconnect myself from those Evangelical Christians who I knew and some who claimed to have been my friends and brethren in the faith. I felt that I was betrayed by those around me. Sometimes I felt family members separated themselves from me. At times, I felt that I was in a lonely place. I remember Judas Iscariot when he betrayed Jesus. This was the one that Jesus called "friend." I believe that Judas was closer to Jesus than the other disciples, but Peter, James, and John had a deeper understanding in the sense of what Jesus revealed to them. It is usually the one closest to us who hurts us the most. When one embarks on a faith journey, there is no turning back. I began to understand why Jesus said "count the cost" (Luke 14:16-18).

The words of the Jehovah's Witnesses echoed in my spirit when they showed me the gospel of Matthew. Jesus said: "Do not think that I came to bring peace on earth. I did come to bring peace but a sword. I have come to set man against his father, a daughter against her mother, and a daughter-in-law against her mother-in-law; and a man's enemies will be those of his own household. He who loves his father or mother more than Me is not worthy of Me. And he who loves son or daughter more than Me is not worthy of Me" (Matthew 10:34-37, NKJV).

Jesus did also say that one must take up His cross and follow Him in verse. Following Jesus means to suffer with Him. The narrow road is hard. When it comes to the ultimatum, one must decide to be rejected by men or be denied by the Son of Man (Matthew 10:32, 33). The Jehovah's Witnesses told me, a long time ago, that, if I were to follow Jehovah, then I would have had to separate myself from the people and those things that would keep me from Jehovah. I learned that there is no friend like Jesus. Jesus said: "If the world hates you, realize that it hated me first. If you belong to the world, the world would love its own; but because you do not belong to the world, the world hates you" (John 15:18-19, The Catholic Bible, NAB).

Discernment means identifying what is God's sovereign will. The way to do that is through detachment, prayer, and journey. Paul said: "Do not conform yourselves to this age but be transformed by the renewal of your mind, that you may discern what is the will of God, what is good and pleasing and perfect" (Romans 12:2 NAB). The Apostle Peter warns the Church not to return to the way of vice. We would suffer because of righteousness. As long as we long for the righteousness of God, then we would be enemies of the world (1 Peter 3:13-14, NAB). David wrote, "Blessed is the man who walks not in the counsel of the wicked, nor stands in the way of sinners nor sits in company with scoffers" (Psalm 1:1 NAB). Recently I had to detach myself from the company of coworker that I hung out with after work. I am not at liberty to explain what happened, but I can say that God was in the midst. What man meant for evil, God meant for God. I broke what I thought was a special friendship that made me public enemy number one. I knew that I had to detach myself from the company so that I could remain focused on the divine calling.

Catholicism teaches that there is virtue through suffering. The journey means denying oneself to follow Jesus. True, no man can serve two masters; one must love one and hate the other (Matthew 6:24, Luke 16:13). When we embark on our spiritual journey, we carry nothing but our faith. Jesus told his disciples to carry nothing. The Son of man had no place to lay his head (Matthew 8:19-22). I learned a lot from Noah's story. When he sent both the dove and raven to provide evidence for dry land, the raven found a place and settled, while the dove returned to Noah with a fig. The dove was weary, but its faith and obedience brought him back safely. In this world, there is no rest for the weary. We are like Abraham who was a sojourner (Genesis 14). Hebrew people, according to one of my late professors, were landless people. This land is not ours; we are only passing through. Our citizenship is in heaven (Philippians 3:20).

The sacrament of grace begins at confirmation. We are baptized into the family of God through the Holy Spirit. The sacraments of Baptism and the Eucharist are taken at confirmation at the end of the conversion process. Conversion is the beginning. Grace is the beginning of the creation for all those who are baptized in Christ.[55]

---

[55] A Guide to the Sacrament of Penance, 2002. http://com/library/Bishops/Guidepen.Htm

Chapter Twelve
Catholic Mediations & Acts of Contrition

The Rosary

I STRUGGLED WITH THE ROSARY for some time. God helped me through this obstacle. The faith is not in the rosary, but in God. Mary was my biggest obstacle. I was ashamed at first to acknowledge it before people. Later, I learned not to allow people to dictate my belief. Only God is my judge, and He decides my fate not Protestants or Catholics. God is truly right and just and not man.

I watched Mother Angelica's series and saw her praying the rosary. The rosary was not a vain repetitious and mindless prayer. It was a verse quoted passage in Luke 1. Mary was only an intercessor, not a goddess. The rosary is not the worship of Mary, nor is the rosary a pagan satanic séance. The rosary is not necromancy (communication with the dead, but the living). The rosary is not voodoo. Saul went to a medium or witch to bring back the Prophet Samuel from the dead, which was forbidden to Israel (1 Samuel 28:7; Leviticus 20:27; Deuteronomy 18:11-14). The rosary is not to conjure up evil spirits. I believe that God answers prayer through Mary. The rosary is only an aide, not the end in itself. When Catholics pray the rosary, they are really reciting the events of the life and ministry of Jesus from the annunciation of Gabriel speaking to Mary to the ascension of Jesus Christ in heaven (Glorious Assumption). Luke 1 begins with the salutation. Mary was blessed and highly favored among women, and the fruit of her womb was Jesus. Therefore, Mary was never the object of worship.

I bought an icon of Saint Michael conquering Satan. I look to it is as a reminder of Christ conquering death and the grave. I learned that Saint Michael was our Prince. Michael is our Protector. He is the War Angel who fights for the Church of Christ because God gave him charge over His people. The angels were always our guardians. We never worshiped the angels, but we could call on them for aide in all areas of life.

Each angel possesses and is named after an attribute of God, such as Jireh (the Lord, our Provider), Shalom (the Lord, our Peace), Nissi (the Lord, our Banner), and Rapha (the Lord, our Healer). David wrote in Psalm 23 that goodness and mercy shall follow us all the days of our lives. These were the angels of goodness and mercy that were given charge over him. God protects us. One author said: "Once I have the canopy of protection built around my property, I maintain it on a regular basis, the presence of darkness is always trying to violate my space. I have to run constant security checks and pray that God will seal up any breaches."[56] We, priest and laity, all alike were required to take authority over every place where the soles of our feet tread.[57]

Warfare requires spiritual drive. If we allow the enemy to take our drive to fight and continue on the journey, then the demons will come in to not attack but destroy us. Jesus warned his disciples that the enemy came to steal, to kill, and to destroy (John 10:10). Jesus provided the way we should pray. The Lord's Prayer sums up every believer's needs and petitions (Matthew 6).

---

56 Robert Abel. <u>The Catholic Warrior</u>. (Denver CO: Valentine Publishing House, 2004). 64
57 Ibid.,65

What is the purpose of prayer? Prayer is the way we have access to God through faith. Faith is the key. Without faith, it is impossible to please God (Heb.11:6) Prayer is essential. "It is through the power of prayer that God is able to show us these issues and help us break them. Prayer not only protects us from generationally inherited curses, but it also has the power to release God's blessings into our lives."[58] A vain prayer is a prayer without faith. I discovered, through prayer, that we have the power to bind and loose in our lives those things that come against us. I learned as a Catholic to pray more. I was told by my ministers in the Evangelical churches to pray more. I will say the Pentecostal denominations do pray a whole lot but in the ecstatic way, unlike Catholic prayer and meditation. I do believe in prayer language, but the power of faith is where the binding and loosing take place. Speaking in tongues or prayer language does help and is important, but we can also pray in our own tongue. Atmosphere is very important. "Pray in secret," Jesus said (Matthew 6:6). There has to be quiet and private time to pray. Many Catholics, not all, do devote themselves to prayer. We ask God to teach us how to pray with our whole being.

Prayer enables us to develop internal senses. We can use outer senses daily. We can recall them in our memory. We can worship God with our intellect. We cannot meditate on what we do not know. "The intellect is the faculty by which man knows the truth; its scope is indicated by its power of knowing abstract truths, relations, universal ideas, etc."[59] Also one must have an appetite to love God. The will is the intellectual appetite that enables us to love objects. The will is a free faculty.[60] We can

---

58 Robert Abel. The Healing Power of Jesus. (Denver, CO: Valentine Publishing House, 2006). 61
59 Eugene Boylan. <u>Difficulties In Mental Prayer</u>. (Princeton, NJ : Scepter Publishers, 1997). 22
60 Ibid.23

use our imaginations to project an image in our minds, yet since we are in a corrupt world, our imaginations can become corrupted.

Paul said that we are to think on things that are pure, holy, noble, just, good, etc. We must worship God with a clear conscience (Philippians 4:8). The mind is the seat of the conscience, and it must be girded with the helmet of salvation. Since we are in a spiritual battle, the weapons are not carnal. We must enable the Holy Spirit to develop us internally by making us prudent in our spiritual walk. Throughout the week, a Catholic goes in to pray and meditate from ten to thirty minutes even to an hour. Not all Catholics pray the Rosary. Catholics do pray directly to saints for help. One can go to God directly. Jesus went directly to the Father, but others can pray for us as well. Some folk do not know how to go to God for themselves. In fact, many Evangelicals I have met would tell me to pray for them. I can step in as an intercessor for them. Mary and the saints are not dead. They are alive in heaven. Prayer is a means of tapping your human energies for creative spiritual purposes. Prayer is a way for one to ground him or herself for empowerment. I will ask this question. Are Catholics the only ones who have the power to tap into the spiritual realm for empowerment? No, any Christian has the power to pray for empowerment. The Rosary was just a way and method of meditation.

Joyful Mysteries on Mondays and Saturdays
The Annunciation; the Visitation; the Nativity Presentation; finding Jesus in the Temple (This section meditates on the Holy Spirit resting upon Mary, the birth of Jesus, and His ministerial awareness at an early age.)

Luminous Mysteries Thursdays
His Baptism in the Jordan; His Self-Manifestation at the Wedding in Cana; His Proclamation of the kingdom of God; with His Call to Conversion; His Transfiguration;

His Institution of the Eucharist and His Paschal Mystery. (This section meditates on the Jesus earthly call to Ministry. Mary confirms Jesus's Ministry; Jesus discloses His divinity to his disciples; Jesus becomes the actual body and blood.)

Sorrowful Mysteries on Tuesdays and Fridays
The Agony in the Garden; the Scourging at the Pillar; the Crowning of the thorns, the Carrying of the Cross, and the Crucifixion. (This section meditates on the arrest, trial, suffering, death, and burial of Jesus as the sacrificial Lamb.)

Glorious Mysteries on Wednesdays and Sundays
The Resurrection; the Ascension; the Decent of the Holy Spirit; the Assumption; the Crowning of the Blessed Virgin.[61] (This section meditates on the glorious resurrection and ascension of Jesus, His crowning glory, and sovereign kingship, along with Mary's ascension.)

Chaplet of Divine Mercy

The priest says, "For the sake of his sorrowful passions, have mercy on us and on the whole world." Catholics recite and sing this Chaplet of Divine Mercy. When we Catholics pray the Rosary, we meditate on the mystery of the passion of the cross which reminds us of the terrible suffering Jesus endured for us. We wore the crucifix as a reminder of the passion He had for us while dying for us. There are some non-Catholics who believe that Catholics do not believe or emphasize the resurrection of Christ. On the contrary, Catholics believe both, and the Rosary

---

61 Loyola Press Jesuit Ministry, 2013, Four sets by John Paul II in 2002. From Website

emphasizes both the death and resurrection. How could Catholicism be a pagan faith when her whole entire liturgy is centered on Jesus Christ?

Before I was confirmed, I became convinced that Catholicism was not a pagan faith. The Mass and the Rosary were definitely not superstition. There were some Catholics who were not comfortable with praying to Mary or the Rosary. I admitted that I did not fully understand the whole mystery of the Rosary. I did have the basics of validity of honoring Mary as Intercessor. Without Mary, there would not have been a Christ. Without the body and blood of Christ, there would be no Mass. By faith, I embraced the mystery of the faith without understanding it. The Holy Spirit had to reveal bits and pieces at a time to me.

Catholics sing or recite, depending on the Catholic parish in the Mass. When we eat this bread and drink this cup, we proclaim your death, O Lord, until you come again. These are not mindless rituals, or vain repetitious sayings. These sayings have life in them. The same is true for the Rosary. "The Rosary" is not a mindless prayer. In the Rosary, Mary and her Son respond to us. The Rosary is not worship, but a prayer and a way to meditate on the mysteries of the passion of Christ. Every time we Catholics partake in the body and blood of Christ, we always prayed: Lord, I am not worthy that I should enter under your roof. Only say the word, and my soul shall be healed (Matthew 8:8). This was from the Centurion.

We say the Lord's Prayer and show a sign of peace to each other before receiving the Mass. The Lord's Prayer was the most popular prayer in Scripture. Jesus showed us how to pray. The petitions were made to Father. True, Jesus never said pray to Mary. The Protestants use this argument to say that Jesus was the Mediator between God and man. Non-Trinitarians argue that we did not pray or worship the Son, but prayer and worship were directly to the Father. Through Jesus all petitions are answered. The saints were constantly praying in heaven, the cloud of witnesses (Hebrews 12:1).

"Our Father who art in heaven" means entering covenantal petition. The Heavenly Father is Our Father who calls us His sons and daughters. We pray as family in the covenant, not as slaves who reverence their master. "Hallowed be Your name" means God's name is "Holy and Sacred" and must be held in high regards as sanctity. The third commandment is not to take or use the Lord's name in vain. "His kingdom come and His will be done on earth as it is in heaven" means that God changes our will so that it will be in harmony with His will. God's purpose is fulfilled in and through us through the Holy Spirit. "Give us this day our daily bread" means that God as our Father supplies all our needs because he is Jehovah-Jireh (The Lord, Our Provider). He is the Bread of Life, who gives himself to us as his food to eat through the Mass. "Forgive us of our trespasses as we forgive those who trespass against us" means that we ask God to enable us to become perfect, just as He is perfect. We are to imitate God's mercy by expressing it toward those who sin against us. We ask for God's mercy, and at the same time, we show mercy to our offenders like in the "Parable of the Unforgiving Servant." Just as the debtor petitions the king for mercy, we are to do likewise in order to bring healing and life to our souls (Matthew 18:21-35). "Lead us not into temptation, but deliver us from evil" means that we ask God not to lead us into trials, not in the sense of seducing or enticement (Matthew 6:13). As we go through trials, we ask God to help us to overcome without succumbing to evil.[62] We end the prayer with "for the kingdom and the power is now yours forever, Amen."

---

62 Scott Hahn. The Lord's Prayer, (Lighthouse Catholic Media, 2011), CD.

In conclusion, the Priest says, "May the Lord be with you." The Congregation responds, "And with your spirit." The Priest says, "We lift our hearts." The Congregation says, "We lift them up to the Lord." The Priest says, "He is truly right and just." Finally, we show a sign of peace to one another.

The Stations of the Cross

In every Catholic Church I have ever entered I have noticed that Jesus is always in the center, not Mary or Joseph, who were on his left and right. The focus was the altar, which was the most holy place in the sanctuary. The image was the crucifix with the body of Jesus on it. Once a Catholic understands that it is not idolatry, then he or she will be able to focus or meditate on the Mystery Passion of Christ. Jesus was the center and object of worship.

True, the second commandment taught that Israel was not to make graven images and bow down to them. Catholics have been criticized for bowing down, not only to icons, but to images as well. Some Christian groups believe that Catholics are idolaters. Catholics are not bowing down to mere imagery like Pagans did in ancient times, but some of the images serve as sacred reminders. Catholics did a whole lot of kneeling in the Mass and the Stations of the Cross. I have done more kneeling in Catholicism than I ever did as a Baptist Evangelical. The Stations of the Cross are fourteen events that explain the passion of Christ. Each piece of art or image explains the events of the trial and the crucifixion. I gained a more vivid understanding of the sorrowful passions of Christ. At each station, there was a homily spoken by the priest, and we bowed to each station, not as an idol worship or graven image, but as a sign of reverence to the one who suffered for us. The Stations of the Cross are not mindless repetitions. It is really up to the individual and how that person understands the mystery of the passion.

Several years ago, a friend of mine, who is now deceased, and I went to see Mel Gibson's The Passion of Christ. I was told that Mel Gibson was Catholic. I did not see how the movie was controversial among some Protestant and Evangelical groups. I heard some preachers and televangelists say that the movie was okay, but the emphasis was not on the resurrection. While my friend and I were watching the movie, what we observed was unbearable for any man to undergo. Of all the Jesus movies I have watched, this one was far more bloody and gruesome. The myth about Catholics not emphasizing the resurrection at all is far from the truth. True, Catholicism does emphasize the suffering of Christ very strongly. That's because we are still in the world, and we suffer and sin daily. We need a Savior interceding on our behalf daily. "Do this in Remembrance of Me," said Jesus. We are celebrating not a memorial, but the Passover. Jesus is our Passover Lamb. Catholics preached both crucifixion and the resurrection of Jesus, but Catholics also celebrate his suffering and resurrection.

There were fourteen Stations of the Cross in each of the Catholic Churches. The Stations of the Cross were ways of teaching us to understand the mystery of the passion. The Stations of the Cross helped us to ponder on what Christ did for us through his suffering. In the liturgy, Catholics repeatedly sing, "For the sake of his sorrowful passion. Have mercy on us and the whole world." Every illustrated picture of the agonies and sufferings of Christ remind me of His love for me. He died for me and you. I moaned, grumbled, complained, and even grew weary at times. Whenever I kneeled before each illustrated image that explained the pain that Jesus suffered from the stripping, the whips, the carrying of the cross, and finally to the cross, I began to reflect on how much He beared for me. The nails that were driven in his hands and feet demonstrated the love He had for me. Isaiah says that surely He has beared our grief, and He carried our sorrows (Isaiah 53:4).

I thought I had completely understood the theology of the humanity and divinity of Christ. After coming back from the Steubenville Bible Conference, more questions and uncertainties rose up because a priest told me that Jesus was human, but we are not. The priest told me that we are inhuman. He said that Jesus was so human that He was able to suffer on the cross as He did because He did not suffer as God, but as man. I agree with him to a certain extent. I agree that Jesus was fully human. Many cult groups would agree, except on the divinity aspect of Jesus. Jesus exemplified what the human ought to be. The theme for the Bible Conference at Franciscan University was Philippians 2:6-9: The Humility of Jesus. Jesus was in the form of God who took on the form of a servant. He did not rob to be equal with God; instead he suffered, died, and rose from the dead, and finally, God exalted Him. Jesus put back on His Glory when God raised Him from the dead. Catholicism never taught that Jesus was Superman. Human logic would say otherwise. If Jesus came into the world as an invincible human being, invulnerable and impeccable, many would consider Him, according to many non-Trinitarian groups and non-Christian religions, to be Superman.

If we could never become what Jesus was on earth, according to the priests that told me this at the conference, then why object Calvinism's Total Depravity that taught that man has no goodness, that the fall of Adam affected the total man, body and spirit? A certain ruler called Jesus a "good teacher." Jesus asked the ruler, why he had called him good? Also, Jesus told a certain ruler that God alone was "good" (Mark 10:18; Luke 18:19). Jesus never claimed to be "good." It did not mean that he was not "good." He was the Image of the Invisible God. Was Jesus pretending not to be good, or did Jesus go undercover by hiding his identity as God?

When I was a Protestant, I was taught that born-again Christians were being conformed to the image of God. If we are inhuman, then it means that we are still in the likeness of Adam since we are subject to death and sin in these mortal bodies (Romans 5). We are being transformed into the image of Christ (2 Corinthians 3:18). I had a dispensationalist minister tell me that we were still in the sixth day being made into the image of God. If man be in Christ, he is a new creature. If we would never become like Christ was on earth, then why did Paul tell the Philippians to imitate Christ? Why did Jesus tell his disciples to be perfect, just as God is perfect, if it were impossible? It is only impossible through human efforts, but through God, all things are possible (Philippians 4:13). There are too many interpretations. Each group condemns each other for its own private interpretations. Many Christians often become confused because there is no absolute interpretation. Each group, including Catholics, claims to have the absolute interpretation based on objective truth, but human beings are limited in understanding.

No wonder the earlier heretics such as Nestorius and Arius objected to Jesus being God and man at the same time, especially Arius. When I was a disciple under the Jehovah's Witnesses, I could see why they objected to Christ being God or God becoming man. The Trinity for many orthodox Christian groups was not the real objection, instead it was the human and divine nature of Christ. The Dualist and the Gnostics objected to Jesus possessing two natures at the same time. Pelagius denied "ancestral sin" (sin nature). The whole point was that Jesus did not have a sinful nature. Jesus resisted temptation and was the spotless Lamb.

I never said that Catholicism was wrong on the matter, but she raised many questions that seemed contradictory. In the Mass, the Body and the Blood, and even water, were both his humanity and divinity. Christianity has always been a complex and complicated faith. It has always been controversial. I did believe in his humanity and his divinity, but I still failed to understand the impeccability of Jesus not being able to sin through freewill. I was taught, as a Protestant, that he was able, yet did not sin. I read many Catholic websites that said that it was impossible for Jesus to sin or to freely choose to sin. Jehovah's Witnesses taught me that Adam and Jesus were human. If Jesus was divine, then Adam was divine because he was perfect. Adam and Jesus were equivalent, yet Jesus was Michael the Archangel before coming into the earth. Jehovah's Witnesses said that it was not God who sinned, but it was man who sinned.[63]

Jesus was the Only Begotten Son conceived by the Holy Spirit without intercourse. Adam was created from the dust, but God breathed His divine essence into his soul. Adam was not conceived but made. Luke stated that Adam was the son of God as well, but Adam was not God (Luke 3:38). Jesus was God (Torah) (John 1:1; Genesis 1:1). God, the Father, did not procreate because He was Spirit. Here is the question: Did Jesus have freewill? It was clear that Jesus had a human will. Jesus never followed his own will. I agree that his human will was not sinful. If He had followed his own will, then He would not have been obedient to the Father, unless His will was in harmony with his Father's will. Jesus prayed to the Father, not for His own will to be done, but for His Father's will to be done (Matthew 26:39; Luke 22:42). That was why Jesus had to stay in constant prayer. Jesus took off his glory, according to Church tradition. However, He ministered as man with a divine nature because He did not come to be served, but to serve. Finite reasoning would say it would have been pointless for Him to have been baptized with the Spirit when Jesus could have displayed His power apart from baptism. He did display divine wisdom at an early age. No miracles were recorded until He was baptized with the Holy Spirit in the river Jordan.

---

63 Should You Believe in the Trinity (Watchtower Tract Society)

There were some Protestant scholars who believed that Jesus did not minister as God, but as man under the framework of the Holy Spirit. Jesus was the reflection and expression of the Father. All groups agree on this, but not all groups are convinced that He was God. Jesus told Philip: "If you seen me, you have seen the Father." The Heavenly Father, God, had to remain in eternity or He would have ceased to have been God (John 14:19). Jesus came as the Lamb of God. Jesus's body was perfect, without defect. His blood was untainted, but pure. The Father provided him a body. Jesus did not provide himself. That was clear. Jesus worshipped the Father and was obedient. Jesus told this to Satan. Jesus did not adore Himself, not as God as man. Jesus revealed His pre-existent nature when He implied several times in the Gospel of John "I Am." Non-Trinitarians argued with me that it was not Jesus speaking but the Torah. The Torah was the Word (Logos).

Penance & Indulgences

This topic was very controversial among Church groups. Salvation was and still is very controversial. All Christian groups believe that there is no salvation apart from the grace of God, outside of Jesus Christ, the Ultimate Sacrificial Lamb, and the Jesus's bodily resurrection from the dead. Non-Catholic groups objected to the concept of penance and the other sacraments as the means for salvation. Earlier I said that I grew up in a Church that had altar calls. I was a Baptist minister who aided pastors by ministering to unsaved folk at the altar call. I was taught to use the same old line from Romans 9:10. I asked the candidate questions concerning the rule of salvation: "Do you believe the Lord Jesus Christ as the Son of God died for your sins and that God raised him from the dead?" The response was always yes. We told them that they were saved since the people confessed Jesus Christ as their Lord and Savior. Many believed that was all that the person had to do. There was no work or merit deed that could be done. In some Baptist and Fundamental circles, the doctrine of Eternal Security ("once saved, always saved") was taught. In other words, one cannot lose his salvation regardless of how many sins he has committed. One could be out of the will of God, fellowship. There were too many mixed signals among Christian groups. A backslider was still saved, but he had to be restored back into the faith. Some Evangelical groups opposed this doctrine. When I was a Baptist, we, Baptists often were criticized for the doctrine of Eternal Security. Many groups taught that one could lose his salvation or fall from the state of grace (Hebrew 6). Baptists have been criticized for teaching "once saved, always saved."

As a former student of Calvinism, I was taught that mankind was so depraved, that there was no goodness at all in mankind because mankind was sinful by nature. Mankind could never merit or return to right standing with God. If mankind had some goodness in him, then there would be no need for Christ. Semi-Pelegianism was the belief that there was a two-way street where God and man meet halfway called synergism. Monergism is the belief that it is God's merits alone that brings mankind back into the state of grace. There are some Protestant groups that believe that salvation is by faith and grace alone, yet one can fall into apostasy. Some Protestant groups believe in faith and works or mere works alone. There is so much confusion. However, I believe that one can divorce himself or herself from God. This is why Paul and John warned the churches of apostasy (Hebrews 6).

Philippians 2:14 says that we are to work out our own salvation with fear and trembling. Catholic priests that I have talked to have taught that we were saved, we are being saved, and we will be saved. The believer who remains in communion and in status with God until the end of his or her life will be saved. He that endures until the end will be saved

(Matthew 13:18-23; 24:13). Daily we are to examine our hearts before God. The soul has to remain constantly in check. We are responsible for what sins we commit. External penance requires fasting, prayer and almsgiving. In the Old Testament, the Levitical priests always made intercessions and supplications for their people in the tabernacle. The priests were always offering sacrifices and making petitions to God on the behalf of the people. Israel's sins were forgiven through the priests. Priests were never saviors. Only God forgives sins. Priests were only the mediators as God's representatives on earth.

What is the doctrine of Penance? According to the Catechism of the Catholic Church, Penance is the interior conversion of the heart toward God and turning away from sin. The penance sacrament is the liturgical celebration of God's forgiveness of sin of the penitent. Catholicism teaches that penance is necessary for salvation for those who have fallen after baptism. True, only God can forgive sins. Penance is reconciliation with God and the Church. The Apostles and the Church were given the keys to bind and loose on earth through the name of Jesus. Whomever you exclude from your communion will be excluded from the communion with God. Reconciliation with God and reconciliation with the Church are inseparable.[64]

Penance means self-afflicting or self-punishment. It is like going to jail. Although our sins are forgiven, we cannot take the grace of God's forgiveness for granted. We acknowledge and deal with the fact we are guilty in the eyes of God. Christ is our high priest and intercessor. Through Jesus's act of sacrifice and ransom, we can deal with our continual transgressions.

Penance is an act of contrition. It means that one detests all his sins because he dreads the loss of heaven and the pains of hell. When we

---

64 CCC. Articles 980, 1445.

are heartily sorry, it means that we acknowledge that we have offend God who deserves all our love.[65] No one can buy forgiveness. Buying forgiveness through the priest or the Church is unbiblical. Penance is realizing that we are truly sorry. It is a matter of the moral conscience. Penance helps us to amend our lives. The gift of penance is to motivate us to repent and deal with our guilt through the aiding work of the Holy Spirit. The Holy Spirit shows us the degree of sin. The offence can be either to God or toward our neighbor.

The sacrament of Penance is also called the sacrament of forgiveness and reconciliation. Penance is a perpetual act because we constantly sin. Through the priests, God grants pardon and peace. The sacrament of reconciliation is followed by conversion. The Apostle Paul wrote "many among you are weak and sick." Each man Paul said "is to examine himself" (1 Corinthians 11:28-30.) King David said: "Examine me, O Lord, and prove me; try my reins and my heart" (Psalm 26:2). John 20:22-23 says: "Receive the Holy Spirit, if you forgive the sins of any, they are forgiven; if you retain the sins of any, they are retained." Jesus was given the power (keys of heaven) to forgive the sins on earth. His Apostles were given the keys to forgive sins. The Church also had the keys or authority to forgive sins (Matthew 16:18-19). This sacrament of grace is necessary for Catholics and Christians to mature and be in right standing with God. Penance is not merit (works), but rather it is a work through the help of the Holy Spirit. Our salvation is not faith alone, but faith that is expressed through works. Paul said that we are to work out our salvation with fear and trembling. It is all done through humility of the soul (Philippians 2:12). Penance is not finding fault in others, but seeing our own faults and dealing with them. Jesus said remove the beam from your eye before trying to remove it from others (Matthew 7:3-5).

---

65 Pennsylvania Catholic Conference of Bishops. A Guide to the Sacrament of Penance. http://ewtn.com/library/Bishops/ Guidepen.HTM. 2000

Catholicism was often accused of adding to Scripture extra-Biblical practices, according to some non-Catholics, since the Middle Ages. This is believed because Emperor Constantine legalized Christianity. The Roman Church has added to traditions to Scripture, and she has deviated, to a certain extent, from the teachings of the Apostles. Indulgence was one of the most controversial teachings since the Protestant Reformation. Martin Luther was well known for challenging the Roman Catholic Church in Germany in 1517 by nailing the famous Ninety-Five Thesis on the doorpost of the Roman Catholic Church. The priest Tetzel was the grand inquisitor of heresy in Poland, and later he became the commissioner for indulgences. Tetzel was granting indulgences for money to build Saint Peter's Basilica. At the same time, he and the Archbishop of Mainz and Cardinal Albert of Brandenburg were keeping some of the money for themselves. Indulgence was remission of temporal punishment. In other words, the guilt was forgiven (Wikipedia, the Free Encyclopedia website). Catholicism received a bad reputation on this topic.

Indulgences were only applied to temporal, not eternal, sins. According to Catholicism, the Bible indicated that these penalties may remain after the sin has been forgiven and that God lessens these penalties as rewards to those who please Him, since Christ's work could not have been be said to have been supplanted by indulgences. The Church acts as Christ's servant in the application of what He has done for us. Therefore, Christ's work has been done over time and not in one big lump (Philippians 2:12; 1 Peter 1:9).

In the eyes of a Protestant, indulgence means that Christ's sacrifice is not enough to wipe away sin once and for all. Since Christ's work was finished on the cross, there is no need for merits since we cannot repay the debt. Catholicism teaches that Jesus made the Ultimate Sacrifice, but the penance for sins is a continuing process, or we would not have need for an Advocate. The Holy Spirit made holy the body of Christ. The

Holy Spirit convicts the human heart of sin. Since the Torah is to dwell in our hearts, the Holy Spirit reveals to us the Torah (Law) of God, and then He will purify our conscience.

True, humans have freedom of choice. Rather than freewill, freedom of choice is a more suitable term to use because humans have a will. Human will is not really free in the sense of bondage and liberty. Calvinists are right to a certain extent. I have to agree with Luther on some of his arguments against Erasimus's defense of human freewill. I read the book, The Bondage of the Will, as a student of Reformed theology. It is not by our freewill that we are saved, but by our response to God's call, according to faith. Our will is no longer our own. Jesus said, "Let the Father's will be done." Mankind can no longer save himself. The Spirit of God draws the individual. No human merit deed can restore us back to God, except through the grace of God. Grace does not end at confession through faith, according to Romans 9:25. God does not impose His will on any man or woman; instead He bestows His grace through His love. John 3:16 says that "for God so loved the world that He gave His only begotten Son so that all who believe in Him will not perish, but have eternal life." Jesus was God's gift to the world. Through Mary, grace was given to the world. The Angel Gabriel told her that she was full of grace. Grace is given through God while we are journeying through this temporal world. Grace was given to benefit us. Grace is not something we waste. God's grace is always sufficient for us. God's work of grace operates through the sacraments as a means of healing and cultivation.

As a convert of the Catholic faith, I really struggled with the doctrine of purgatory. In the back of my mind, I somewhat believed it, but needed more Scriptural evidence for backing up the claim. Indulgence involves prayers for the dead, especially those who are in purgatory. The only account that records the practice is in 2 Maccabees 39-46. One must purge himself of sin whether here on earth or after death in purgatory. It is clear that purgatory is not hell. I was told by the parish priest that purgatory is a place where those believers who have not gotten rid of all of their sins. That person must go through a very painful process of purification. Grave sins deprive us of our communion with God and make us incapable of eternal life. We know that the Greek word for fire is "Pur." Fire is not always necessary to destroy or to consume something or someone. It actually can mean purge. Since the Holy Spirit is described as fire, He sanctifies us, purifies our conscience. He convicts the human heart of sin. Works are consumed by fire (1 Corinthians 3:13-15; 2 Peter 3:10).

Confession

In the New Testament, it seems much harder to follow God. Jesus presented a more excellent way of salvation, yet a much harder road to take. Jesus taught self-denial. As Christians and as human beings, we strive for perfection, and we contend with sin. True, Jesus made the ultimate sacrifice once and for all. He also sent the Holy Spirit as the Sanctifier, who is to make holy the body. Catholics do not pray to a priest. In the early Church, the Christian community confessed their sins to one another. True, we all can go to God for ourselves since the veil ripped in the Holy of Holies, through which Jesus gave us access to the presence of God. He is the High Priest that has Mediated and Interceded on our behalf throughout all the ages. No priest can offer up the ultimate sacrifice since Jesus has done that for us. Confessing to a priest does not mean that Jesus's sacrifice was in vain. As a Protestant, I went to and did altar calls, and the preacher served as a channel to God proclaiming the "SINNER'S PRAYER" in Romans 10. Yes, Christ has forgiven us of our sins, and He has wiped the slate clean. However, we still sin unintentionally, yet we still must repent of the unintentional sins. The priests receive instruction from Jesus to confirm the forgiveness of sins to the individual. While I was at the Bible Conference, many priests were hearing confessions. I had a Franciscan priest tell me that confession was a place where we bring our dirty laundry and God brings us out of the washer and into the dyer clean. I had never thought about confession in that manner before.

The Advocate helps us to deal with and overcome sinful desires. According to the Pennsylvania Bishops, "Confession is a sacrament instituted by Jesus in his love and mercy. It is here that where we meet loving Jesus who offers sinners forgiveness for offences committed against God and neighbor. At the same time, Confession permits sinners to reconcile with the Church, which is also wounded by our sins." Also, the article said: "Confession is the visible manifestation of God's mercy provided for us, the clear awareness that God has forgiven us."[66] My first trip to the shrine was my first confession. I admit that I was afraid to go to confession without hellfire and brimstone being thrown at me. The Church's job is to scare the hell out of us so that we will not go to hell. The priests always ask: "When was your last confession?" I was told to say ten times "Jesus, I trust in you."

I remembered my second trip back to Hanceville, Alabama. I took a tour through the lower floor sanctuary. I was praying along with the others in the tour group. After I finished praying, I touched the huge crucifix of Christ, and then I touched His pierced side. I was saying in the room alone: "Lord, I am sorry. Please forgive me! I and others do not realize how much we, your bride, hurt you. Your bride has hurt those who have turned away from you." Then later, I went to confession.

One day I went to a confession back home, and I was at a place of resentment and hurt that I had experienced in both the past and the

---

66 A Guide to The Sacrament of Penance, 2000.

present. The priest told me to go to those who had hurt you and forgive them. He told me to do penance by reading Psalm 103 and repenting.

There was another time that I went to confession under the same priest, not my parish priest. I told him that I was on the verge of giving up and that I had begun to lose my spiritual drive for God. The priest told me to go and pray "Our Father" ten times.

Confession is good for the soul. There are some Christians who oppose confessing to a priest for forgiveness of sins. As a former Protestant, I was taught that we can go to God for ourselves. At altar call, many give their testimonies of their conversion experience from the old man to the new man in Christ. The priest and pastors serve as mediators and intercessors for their flock. Many sheep do not know to go to God for themselves. Catholics do not pray to priests; they pray to God. Not all Catholics pray to Mary. Everyone needs an intercessor. Intercessors are not saviors, but servants standing on the behalf of God. Confession enables a believer to release and empty out his painful soul. When one talks to a minister or a priest, the individual is able to express his feelings and spill out his soul.

I wrote a paper and received an "F." I cried and was so upset. I filled out the form to drop the course. One of my seminary professors was a tough teacher. The professor did not want us to tell him about the article itself, but to share our personal experiences relating to the article. The same professor told me, "I want see and read more Andrew in the papers rather than the articles themselves." The same seminary professor, who taught Pastoral Counseling, when writing a paper about a topic that involved counseling, told us to spill out our souls. I had to read a book on the wounded healer written by Henri J.M. Nouwen as required reading. In order for someone else's wounds to heal, we must open up our scar wounds. At first, I found it difficult to open up my personal wounds because I was afraid of judgment and criticism.

Paul told the Church to confess their sins to one another. The purpose of confession is to deal with the venial sin before it becomes a mortal sin. Confession was both touchy and personal. I go to confession every now and then. I go to different parish priests for confession. Catholics are lined up every Saturday afternoon. One of things that God requires of his people as an offering was a broken and contrite spirit. Prayer and confession are the means of relinquishing the soul. We cannot deal with our sins without someone to help us through the process. I can say that confession enables me to acknowledge and deal with the imperfections within my soul. Forgiveness is a major obstacle for me because I hold and suppress so many past sins against those who have offended me. Scott Hahn said that the sins we mainly commit are those we have experienced offence from. The unforgiveness we have comes from deep-seated thoughts, gossiping, and backbiting. I love when Scott Hahn said, "when we do not forgive, we stop breathing spiritually."[67] Confession is a way of letting go and letting God.

Votive Candle of Prayer

A votive candle is a small candle made of red or yellow beeswax. I have seen the blue candles. These are used by individuals who are offering their prayers to God for themselves and for other people. True, there are icons behind the candles. There is a place to kneel and pray. The Virgin Mother is one of the icons prayers are offered up to. Votive Prayer is not worship to the icons, but prayers offered up to God. The saints we asked to intercede for us. When one enters a Catholic Church, one will see that the sanctuary is in the form of the tabernacle. The main altar is the most

---

67 Scott Hahn. CD on "The Lord's Prayer."

holy place in the Catholic Church. Catholics bow to the altar because it represents the divine presence of God where the priest offered up the hosts. The water laver was where we washed our hands when entering the sanctuary. The votive candle was the place we offered up our prayers and supplications before God. Anyone can offer a votive prayer. One does not have to be Catholic to do it. After my conversion I went weekly to a Catholic Church, and I offered up votive prayers. John 8:12; 12:46 says it is a prayer of coming into the light of Christ. The candle itself in beeswax symbolizes the purity of Christ, His human soul, and His divinity, according to medieval tradition.[68] This is no different than the seven lamp stands that are constantly burned by the priest. The lights are never unattended. The oil in the lamps represents the Holy Spirit, and the light is the human soul of man that is to constantly burn.

---

68 Father William Saunders. Shedding Light on the Use of Votive Candles. www.ewtn.com July 14 1994 issue of the "Arlington Herald."

Chapter Thirteen
Catholic Enlightenment

When some people think of religion, they define religion as vain ceremonial practices and man-made traditions that water down God's people with repetitive practices and liturgy. Religion means "way of life." "Religion at its core is the quest for God.... In a special way, this personal quest for God is concentrated in prayer; our personal prayer widens out to join with our fellow brothers and sisters in community prayer."[69] One thing about a spiritual journey is that I am not truly alone. Paul prayed that Ephesus's eyes would be opened to the glorious mysteries of Christ (Ephesians 1:1-13). The deeper I had gone into the Catholic faith, the more the Holy Spirit has begun to open my eyes to the hidden truths. I did what some former Protestants have done. I attempted to investigate the faith by trying to prove that Roman Catholicism was a cult. I went in as an Evangelical, but I came out as a Catholic convert. The more I tried to find errors in the Catholic teachings, the more convinced I became of how right Catholicism was. Paul gave thanksgiving to God for opening up the eyes of the churches to the glorious mysteries of Christ. Enlightenment was a way of saying the God has enlightened His people through revelation. New Age Enlightenment was rationalism and humanism, which denied God and rejected His assistance. Vain philosophies never ensured salvation because they did not produce

---
69 Cardinal Donald Wuerl. New Evangelization. (Huntington, IN: Our Sunday Visitor Publishing Co., 2013).65

eternal life (Colossians 2:12). This was the wisdom of the world. Philosophy was never in itself, but it never contained revelation. The wisdom of the world rejects the foolish wisdom of Christ because it does understand the deep things of God (1 Corinthians 1:18-31). The term enlightenment has received a bad reputation for over a few centuries. Enlightenment just means "opening the eyes."

When Paul wrote to Timothy, he said that he had been taught, since infancy, that sacred Scriptures were capable of giving him wisdom for salvation through faith in Jesus Christ (2 Timothy 3:15). One may think he has eternal life by studying the Scripture, but Jesus confirmed that the Scriptures spoke of Him (John 5:39). Jesus said to the unbelieving Jews that their belief that Scriptures have life in them was not enough for salvation because they had rejected Him. People who always studied and learned were never able to come to the knowledge of the truth (2 Timothy 3:7).

Since I was twenty years old, I have been on a journey, forever searching, but I have always ended up in circles. The more I have searched, the more questions have risen up. Solomon said that a person who studies many books exhaustively wears out his flesh (Ecclesiastes 12:12). Archbishop Fulton Sheen said it best. He said: "People with an infernal pride will sometimes take the lowest places in order to attract attention; so often those who boast that their minds are in a state of suspension until they find truth are often those who are most impervious to it ... Search for the truth but not to find it; they love the chase but not for the capture; they admire the footprints of truth, but not catching up with it. They go through life talking about 'widening the horizons of the truth' but without ever seeing the sun."[70] The truth does, however, bring us into the state of humility. Paul said the knowledge was puffed up (1 Corinthians 8:1). When one

---

[70] Fulton J. Sheen. Way to Inner Peace. (New York, NY: Society of Saint Paul, 1995). 154-155

puffs himself up with knowledge, he usually prostitutes his arrogance to people. There are people who hate hearing and knowing the truth. The truth hurts. The truth makes us free (John 8:38). There are those who love to collect abstract truth, but never embrace it. One can love truth, yet not know how to handle the truth. The truth always shows us up. The truth can be ugly and scary. One is accountable for the truth after revealing it. Truth brings accountability. Face to face, the truth brings us into the light. The truth is not to inflict pain, but to heal us and draw us closer to God. The truth involves a painful process. The Spirit of Truth convicts the heart of sin and of righteousness (John 16:8). As the Spirit of Truth convicts the heart of sin, the Spirit also is our Advocator who Jesus called the Helper. We cannot do it alone! No man is an island to himself; he needs his neighbor to help him along. This is the Creator's design.

I believe that, if Protestants even tried to understand some of the mystery in the teachings of the Church, that many of the dilemmas within churches, such as marital, family, community, and moral issues could be reduced or eradicated. The people of God are destroying themselves due to the lack of knowledge as a whole. The Church is following the same path that Israel and Judah did.

Strength comes in numbers, all the Church body has to do is work together and cultivate its members from within. However, this does not mean that we, Catholics and denominations, will ever come into one union on the surface, but we all can come into a union internally which is spiritual.

Catholic enlightenment is on a personal basis as well as corporate one. Each person is to embark on a spiritual journey through means of meditation, devotion, and prayer. Although Catholicism (Christianity) and Buddhism are two completely opposite faiths, both do seek enlightenment, but in different ways. I am not saying that all religions lead to God, but most of the religions have common universal axioms.

I have a great respect for Catholicism because she respects the universal axioms, or general truths, among religions without deviating from her core stance on the teachings of Jesus and His Apostles. Catholic enlightenment, according to my personal experience, means drawing closer to God. My ultimate pursuit is not intellectual, but rather it is to enter into the divine presence of God. All I sought was confirmation and that God was with me. Every time I went to the Church, I prayed and hoped to make the connection with God like the saints did. What Catholic enlightenment taught me was to learn how to focus on the mysteries of the Incarnation of the Word. When I embarked on pilgrimages, the pictures and icons enabled me to contemplate deeply on the life, death, and resurrection of Jesus Christ. When Jesus said, "Do this in remembrance of me," He was saying along with the Passover and Unleavened bread.

Knowledge of God was revealed to me in bits and pieces through many Christian faiths. Each faith geared me up for spiritual battle. I learned not to be antagonistic toward Christian faiths, even the cults, because God can use any faith to equip His people in the knowledge of His Son. I admitted there are faiths that are more sound than others, but even some truth or little insight helped me to catch a tiny glimpse of God's truth. There are many things that we will never understand about the mystery of Christ until we see him face to face. God knew we could not handle the whole truth. There is a difference between absolute truth and the whole truth. God's Spirit has to give us bits and pieces at a time. Until then, we only see and know in part what Apostle Paul said (1 Corinthians 13).

The Shrine of the Most Blessed Mother
The Hanceville, Alabama Pilgrimage

After I was confirmed into the Catholic Faith, I needed inspiration. I was a seeker who sought truth and enlightenment. I felt that my eyes needed to be opened more to Catholicism because there were still remaining uncertainties about the faith and my decision to convert to Catholicism. For many years, I found myself wavering. I knew that I needed a strong, solid foundation. Thank God for the priest. The whole purpose for the journey was to give me motivation. One year ago, I went to Birmingham, Alabama, to the EWTN studio. I met several celebrities at the studio. During my pilgrimage in Birmingham, Alabama, there were fellow Catholics who helped me out by advising me and encouraging me to continue embarking on the Catholic journey. Catholics stick together. I had been confirmed shortly before taking the trip. Throughout the pilgrimage, I learned to value and appreciate Catholicism even more. Unlike some Christian sects, many Catholics helped one another though the spiritual process, especially those who were embarking on a spiritual journey. If I have to choose a theme for Catholicism, it would be the faith journey. Catholicism to a Catholic is about the journey. One's calling is a journey. One day, I would like to visit Rome, but the journey I long to happen in my lifetime is to go to Jerusalem. So far the best pilgrimage that I have ever taken was the "Shrine of the Most Blessed Mother." This place was where I felt God's presence the most. It was a getaway place, rather than a vacation.

There is no commandment or requirement to make spiritual pilgrimages. Muslims make their hajj to Mecca yearly. Jews go to the Wailing Wall in Jerusalem. There is no harm in making pilgrimages. I remembered one of my professors saying that religion was attractive. In reference to Catholicism, the statement is true. Catholics are taught through visual means (symbols, arts, and relics). Visual symbols help one to understand his or her Christian faith more clearly. A few months ago, I revisited the site for more spiritual insight and meditation. Hanceville, Alabama's "Shrine of the Most Blessed Mother" enabled me to clear my thoughts and to ponder on the deep things of God through mediation.

Catholics have always been people of prayer. Catholics prayed corporately and individually. The symbols at the shrine helped me to meditate.

The best part of the trip was the "Pope John Paul II Museum." It was like taking a tour through the Atlanta aquarium, the King Center, or through a dinosaur museum. The friar was telling the story of each relic and picture in John Paul II's life and his teachings. The museum at the shrine had history of the Reformation and works and icons of the Church Fathers like Augustine and Thomas Aquinas, and there was a room that had many icons of Christian martyrs throughout Church History and their testimonies, the Apostles and even the films on the Eucharist. After this tour was over, I was so inspired that I did not want to leave the place.

After the Easter Vigil, I knew I was embarking on a new journey after completing one journey. The journey was struggling to remain Catholic. The parish priest said to the new converts that the devil will attack and tempt us. He told us to always remain in the fellowship. I realized that I could not do it alone. The battle was spiritual. I knew that I had to deepen my prayer, devotion, and meditation. Maturity is a must. I knew that I had an Advocate (Holy Spirit), who would help me through the growth process and the journey. At times I found myself wavering in my faith, so the pilgrimages and scenery reminded me of God's peace and presence. Intellectually, I have developed a whole lot, but morally and spiritually needed catching up. Sometimes I went to the Church downtown, which was more sophisticated and formal, yet it had beautiful outdoor scenery that helped me meditate. I preferred the scenery over the sanctuary because I felt too confined. I would carry my rosary around through the outside scenery. I was always a child of scenery. And no matter how beautiful the Church's scenery was, it was nothing compared to the splendor of the shrine in Alabama. The sole reason why I left the Baptist denomination was because I was not challenged theologically and spiritually. When I went on the trip, I saw the wealth and treasures in the Catholic arts and icons. After making two trips to the shrine, my Catholic faith seemed to grow even stronger. As a matter of fact, I know it did.

The Monastery of the Holy Spirit Pilgrimage in Conyers, Georgia

This was the first time that I ever visited a monastery. Friars and nuns were often criticized and misunderstood as being close-minded to the realities of the world. This was far from the truth. True, friars and nuns vowed to renounce the world and its materialism to serve God wholeheartedly. These nuns and friars lived simple lives. Not all were called to the order of monastic life. These groups of people taught me the art of humility as well as self-denial. When these brothers and sisters prayed and meditated, they placed others above themselves. My parish priest was Franciscan. The Monastery of the Holy Spirit was the friar of the Trappist order.

While I was in Conyers, Georgia, I went to the Monastery of the Holy Spirit. I believe in getting away. A monastery or a pilgrimage was like the calm center of the hurricane. The storm represented chaos. The world in which we live is filled with chaos and disorder. Pilgrimages are places designed for all believers to rebound and regain their senses and sanity. The monasteries were a retreat. A retreat is not cowardice; it is a place where God can minister to the souls and strengthen his people. Retreats to monasteries do not get one into heaven, but they serve as a means of preserving the soul from perishing. A retreat is timeout with God. I see it as a place and time for a breath of fresh air.

Catholicism taught that one was to make time for God. Take time out of our busy schedule. Reading passages of Scripture, singing hymns to the Lord in secret, as well as in public. Jesus said, "Pray in secret." Prayer and meditation were gifts given from God to benefit us. The body is the shell of expression. We utter from the soul. All that is within us is what makes us beautiful in the eyes of God. Our natural surroundings are splendid, but not as splendid as human dignity. Our soul is made up of three primary powers (mind, reason, and will), and two secondary powers (imagination and sensuality). When we read devotional books, we see the word yourself.[71] As Catholics, we worship God, not only with our spirit but also with our senses. The spirit man is only the core of our outer man.

God does not impose His will on any man. However, if He chooses a person to carry out his work, God will see to it that His will will be carried out. God gave us not only freewill, but He also gave us the innate ability to respond. We freely go to God. God wants us to freely come to him. "We pray with our will whenever we go to prayer, in accordance with God's will, and put ourselves in a suitable attitude of body, turning our mind, as far as we can, away from all else but God, and endeavoring to persevere in that mind and body." [72]

We ask that God bestows His grace upon us so that His Spirit can work through our will to approach Him. When we approach God, faith is required of us. Faith is the breath of spiritual life, the substance of things we hope for, the evidence of things that appear not. Faith is, therefore, of capital importance.[73]

---

71 Bernard Bangley. The Cloud of the Unknowing. (Brewster, MA: Paraclete Press, 2006). Chapter 62
72 M. Eugene Boylan. Difficulties in Mental Prayer. (Princeton, NJ: Scepter Publishers, 1997). 140
73 Ibid.,145

One thing I learned in the Reformed Churches was silence. I grew up in a Church setting that was noisy. Music was great and so was shouting and dancing which were all adoration to the Creator Himself. However, silence is a way to contemplate on the things of God. When we are silent, God is speaking. Paul said whatsoever things which are noble, just, pure, and lovely and of good report we are to think on these things (Philippians 4:8). David had an ascetic spirit. He was disciplined in his meditation in spite of his shortcomings. When he entered into the most holy place, he always prostrated before the altar, meditating on the law and precepts of God (Psalm 119). David was a man after God's own heart because David diligently sought Him. David's mind was always on God.

The power of meditation enables us to focus on the Creator himself through His marvelous works (Psalm 19:1). Meditation means to ponder upon, and it also means to utter out loud. Day and night, the faithful are to meditate on the Lord (Psalm 1:1). "To ponder is to silently sit with what we cannot comprehend. Meditation embodies of what we cannot comprehend. As we sit in meditation, attentive to our bodily stillness, we cannot comprehend all that our body stillness really is ... Sitting in incomprehensibility of ourselves and everything around us, we incomprehensively find our way through the gate into all that lies within."[74] When we enter into God's presence, we enter not knowing so that he may reveal to us what we do not comprehend. After all, God is Incomprehensible. Meditation does not always involve cloisters, but monasteries without walls. One can meditate in the fields where there is scenery. Catholicism was known for both architecture and scenery. I learned to experience God through our surroundings. Did not Saint Francis of Assisi adorn God through nature, always out in the fields?

---

74 James Finley. Christian Meditation. (New York, NY: Harper One, 2004).112

God was never confined to a wall. In the Old Testament, God dwelt in the "Ark of the Covenant," then later God no longer dwelled in a temple, but rather in the hearts of His people. Meditation involves the flowing of thoughts we experience which is not an adversary. Mediation is not the bad guy. In other words, Christians should not fear meditation. Meditation has been given a bad reputation. Some people mistake meditation with mysticism. It is important to meditate without distractions.[75] Meditation is not chanting. Meditating is pondering on the works of God through creation (Psalm 19:1). When we meditate, we focus on the present moment with God because God is Ever-Present.

One fascinating thing about meditation is that it is universal, but the downside of mediation is the way one meditates, especially in religions. Buddhists and Hindus meditate constantly. Islam prays so many times a day in meditation. It is obvious that God placed an innate ability in humans to meditate, but the enemy has blinded the minds so that people cannot mediate on the Maker. Romans 1 clearly explains that the Gentiles worship the creature rather than the Creator. In spite of the Gentiles' spiritual blindness, one must admire their discipline. Christian meditation is oneness with God, rather than oneness with self and nature.

The mind requires a whole lot of discipline because it is the seat of human conscience. The mind can be either a pure or a dirty instrument based on the individual's thought patterns. A priest told me at my first confession in Alabama that, whatever a man thinks, so is he. The mind had to be purged of dirty thoughts and trained to attain pure thoughts. The mind is the hardest instrument to master. The mind is a very powerful instrument that is delicate and fragile like the heart. Paul mentioned the whole armor of God, and one of the gears was the helmet of salvation. I listen to Joyce Meyers all the time. She wrote a book called

---

75 Ibid.,210

The Battlefield of the Mind. The mind is the battlefield where the enemy wages war.

As we pray and meditate, the Spirit enables us to relinquish those things that hinders us from the presence of God. David said, in Psalm 1:1, "Not only the man who is blessed walks not in the council of the ungodly nor standing in the way of sinners, nor the seat of the scornful, but he will meditate on him day and night." Psalm 119 is filled with meditations. I admit that I was easily distracted. Jesus resisted temptation by remaining obedient through prayer and meditation. Time of meditation was given to us for our own benefit as grace from God. God will give us perfect peace if our mind stays on Him (Isaiah 26:3).

In conclusion, the thing that God requires the most is a broken and contrite spirit. David was the epitome of one who came before God with a broken and contrite spirit (Psalm 51). Fear is God's delight. God wants His children to make time for Him. My whole point is to make time for the Lord our Creator. Take about ten to fifteen minutes on a nice day and ponder on the handiwork of God, and adore Him for His accomplishments (Psalm 19:1).

The Steubenville, Ohio, 2015 Bible Conference

I was blessed with the opportunity to go to Franciscan University in Steubenville, Ohio. For months I was excited about the conference, and I finally met Scott Hahn. I had listened to Scott Hahn on EWTN. I was fascinated with his thorough knowledge of the Scriptures. He was one of the few Bible teachers that brought the Scriptures into light with clarity. I was impressed with his Old Testament historical knowledge through Catholic lenses.

I faced some obstacles before the trip. The enemy was surely testing me. I knew that he did not want me to go to the conference. The car I had bought a year before decided to breakdown. The computer and coils and other parts of the car decided to tear up. I was frustrated because it took all the money I had saved up for the trip to fix it. What the warranty did not cover I had to pay for. I asked the Lord if He wanted me to go on the trip or not? Was it meant to be?

I was glad that God was watching after me. If I had gone on the trip before the car problems, I would have been stranded on the road. On my way to the conference, I went through some rough roads. I had used tires I had gotten a month prior to the trip, good tires. When I left South Carolina, everything was fine. When I arrived in Charleston, West Virginia, my front tires began to slide in the thunderstorm. The roads were so bad that I thought I had a blowout, and my hazard lights would not work. I pulled off the exit and into an AutoZone to check my tires. My tires were still somewhat ok, except the tires were at the medial point of the tread which concerned me. When I arrived in Pittsburgh, I was safe. I could not rest because I had little money. I had just enough money for the hotel and gas. I was so upset because I needed new tires for the front. I had to use my overdraft to get brand new tires. I was so upset. I was so upset with God because I felt that my trip was ruined.

I arrived at Franciscan University sensing the peace and beauty of the campus. There was no doubt that the spirit of Saint Francis was there. When the conference began, then I began to enjoy the experience of God. My mind was off my problems. The people I met were beautiful people. These Catholics were from all over the country and other parts of the world. At first I feared that ostracism would be at the conference, but it the opposite. Everyone made me feel welcome. This was the first time that I felt a part of true spiritual family. In my heart, I said: "I felt, at that time, that I belonged in Catholicism." I ate lunch and dinner with people that I had never met before. People came to my table. All of us were sharing our Catholic conversion experiences. At last there were people who were on my level of understanding. I could not have or share theological and Biblical views with Catholics at home like I did at the conference. These Catholics were very open-minded. I told them that they were unlike the Catholic Churches in the south, especially in my area. In my hometown, most of the Catholics act more like some of the watered down denominational churches. Some former Protestants said this to me all the time.

The worship in the Catholic Churches in Greenville, South Carolina were so formal, that there was no uplifting in them. My parish was an African-American cultural Catholic Church, but the Steubenville conference had put it to shame. The conference was so charismatic that I thought I was back in a Pentecostal Church. The conference brought back my Bible college memories, which were Pentecostal. I felt, at that moment, homesick for my home Baptist Church which was Charismatic. We worshipped as one entity. The Spirit moved in that conference. The lectures were great, but not as great as the praise and worship. Experiencing God's presence was what I sought. I had spent many years seeking to make this connection with God. The spirit of Saint Francis was there at the conference. I saw elderly people, I mean, up in age, lifting up their hands, and some were praying in the Spirit. I took out my camera to take pictures of people lifting up their hands. The atmosphere was so powerful and filled with anointing. The focus was on the Lord Jesus Christ the whole time.

The unity was not a perfect unity, but it was unified enough for God to manifest Himself in the body. I said that this was what the body ought to be. God then made it clear to me that He wanted me to see how He wants his body to be. That was the heart of the trip, not so much the intellectual stimulation. Philippians was the theme of the conference. In

Philippians 3, Paul said that we learn to put those things that are behind us and press toward the mark of the prize of the high calling, perfection. When I left the conference, a spark of motivation flared up in me. I had a new perspective on Catholic spirituality. This was truly Catholic Enlightenment.

After the evening the Holy Hour, I met Jeremiah Hahn, one of Scott Hahn's sons who was studying for the priesthood, and we engaged in a theological conversation. He was impressed with my previous denominational background. I told him how his father was one of the reasons I had become Catholic. I believe, when the Bible says, that no man can come to the Father except through me. This was the case of Jeremiah Hahn. I met the son before I met the father. I said that I could not leave the Bible Conference without meeting Scott Hahn. If I had not met Scott Hahn, I would have been devastated and disappointed because he was the reason that I made the trip. God performed a miracle the next day. All the authors were in the building for a book signing. Guess who was there? It was Scott Hahn! I bought one of his books and approached him. I said: "Gotcha! I have finally Gotcha!" He laughed. I told him where I was from and that he was the reason of my conversion. He grabbed his chest, and he lifted his hands to the Lord, giving him the credit for it all. Hahn said, "It was God who made it possible." I met him again later that night at the Saint Paul Biblical Center of Theology. Everyone gathered around to meet Scott Hahn. Scott Hahn was sharing his experiences and his mother's illness. We prayed over him. I was amazed at this type of Catholicism. He gave me some advice about how to write a book, and we departed.

Chapter Fourteen
Vocational Discernment

When I was in Hanceville, Alabama, the chaplain priest told me, during my first confession, to spend a few years strengthening my faith foundation in Catholicism before choosing a vocation. I admit that I struggled with ten percent of the Catholic teachings, especially on the Holy Orders, one of the seven sacraments in Catholicism. The Latin word is Sacramentum, which means a "sign of the Sacred." The sacraments were ways for us to experience God's presence. The sacraments also served as time signs and instruments of God's grace. The sacraments help believers, especially Catholics to embark on their spiritual journey.[76] The Reformed definition of the Sacraments differed from the Catholic definition. As a student of Reformed theology, I was taught that the sacraments were holy rites that were signs and means of grace. The Augustinian definition taught that the sacrament was a visible sign of an invisible grace. The sacraments are defined as having been instituted by God to serve as external signs (means of elements) to confer on and seal to believers by grace the promise of the gospel for the remission of sins. However, according to the Reformed view, there were only two rites of the church that applied: baptism and the Lord's Supper. The other five

---

76 The Seven Catholic Sacraments, (American Catholic.Org Site from Franciscans and Franciscan Media, 1996-2015)

were not (promissio evangelicae) promised of salvation.[77]

The Seven Sacraments are not means of salvation in themselves, but they are the Christian vocational callings. Baptism, Confirmation, Eucharist, Penance, Anointing of the Sick, Matrimony and Holy Orders are the seven sacraments that were given through Christ Jesus. The sacraments are meant to build up the body of Christ. Overall, it is the Christian Calling that is consecration and devotion to God. We are to offer Spiritual sacrifices to God for our reasonable service (Romans 12:1). Not all vocations apply to us, but most of them do. Not all are called to marriage. The Catholic call means that we no longer belong to ourselves, but now we belong to God.

Vocational calling is self-denial. He, who keeps his life, shall lose his life, but he, who loses his life, shall keep it (Matthew 16:25; Mark 8:35; and Luke 17:33). One must seek to know his or her role in ministry. When I was confirmed into the Catholic Faith two years ago during the Easter Vigil, the priest asked us, the candidates, if we believed everything the Church teaches. In the back of my mind, several questions were raised. I was able to embrace ninety percent of the teachings. However, I trusted the judgment of the Church. I fully agreed with the Apostles Creed and the Athanasian Creed. We all said, "Yes!" I agreed because the creeds were universal. One cannot adsorb over two thousand years of traditional teachings in short period of time. I believed that the Church was the "True Church."

Here comes much of the ten percent that I struggled with. If my subjective conscience did not bother me, I would have easily entered into the priesthood or the deaconate. Truthfully, I was really afraid to make the move because I was uncertain about taking the oath and

---

77 Richard A. Muller. Dictionary of Latin and Greek Theological Terms. (Grand Rapids, MI: Baker Book House Company, 1985). 267-268

about taking on the responsibilities of the clergy. Again, I was raised on "Scripture Alone." I agreed with Scripture, with bishops and deacons being able to marry. Paul wrote to Timothy that both the overseer and the deacon were to be the husband of one wife and to manage his household well (1 Timothy Ch. 2). Protestants, some sects, at least, argued and required that a man must be married before taking on the pastoral role or the deacon role. Yet, many of the ministers who were not ordained like me, who were licensed, were either married or single, ironically. Many denominations have their reasons for the pastor being married. Catholic priests often were stereotyped by some Non-Catholics as practicing sexual immorality. If that were the case, then one could say the same thing about such practices in the Protestant Churches. I cannot get into it for the sake of credibility. I felt that Catholic priests received injustice because of the misconceptions about the single clergy. There were many single, devoted Catholic priests who were totally sold-out to God. There was no actual Scriptural support that I know of for taking the vows of poverty, obedience, and chastity. One can single out passages to justify the formulated doctrine through reasoning.

After the RCIA, I asked a deacon, who was single, what it was like struggling as single man in the office. The deacon told me that he still struggled with the single life of a deacon, and even the married deacons told me that they struggled as married deacons. I spoke to the deacons because it was a male thing. What I mean by this is I learned that priests struggled with sexual desires before and after the vows.

During the RCIA, I asked the parish Franciscan Priests why Catholicism did not promote married priests? The candidates were asking the same questions. One person asked why there was one Catholic priest married who had been Anglican. This RCIA candidate argued that Catholics needed more married priests because a married priest could relate to married couples who are experiencing family and marital issues. I had to agree with the man. A married priest would have been appropriate for marriage and family counseling. The Franciscan priest had put on a defense mechanism at first. The priest did say that a single priest could do what a married priest could do. The parish priest also asked, "Why would a married person take on so much burdensome responsibility, and then have to balance that out between family and Church?" It was an interesting argument for why the single priests could shepherd flocks. Also a single person could obligate his entire time in the ministry without distraction.

Fr. Andrew Apostoli said: "In summary, it is evident that St. Paul encourages celibacy over marriage. But he also emphasizes that this decision must always be made freely. He says that it is not wrong to marry, but he feels that people who marry will have trials in this life, and wants to spare those who, have not yet embraced the married life from these trials (1 Corinthians 7:28)."[78] I believed single priests were capable of doing it all. I really wanted my parish priest to argue from Scripture about why the priests were to be single? Scriptures are refutable from both sides. Obviously, it would be hard to just come from Scripture alone because the Bible does not give a clear, direct answer. The Franciscan parish priest did give a brief history on the early Church. I was amazed with the reasons for single priests. The history was interesting. I had read in seminary that there were women priests until the Church of Rome banned women from being priests. I knew that women were only confined to baptizing other women in the Roman Catholic Church. The parish priest said that, if a bishop or priest divorced his wife, then the wife took half of what the Church owned. The conversation got more interesting when the deaconate candidates jumped in the discussion. I Corinthians 7 is pointed out as the argument for single priest. The

---

[78] Andrew Apostoli. When God asks for an Undivided Heart, Choosing Celibacy in Love and Freedom. (Irving, TX: Basilica Press, 2007). 71

passage does not prove that the priests were to be single. I left it alone for a while. I hesitated to convert because I would have to set aside my ministerial license from another denomination. As a matter of fact, I felt that I was never acknowledged as a minister by other ministers in the Baptist denomination.

True, all people are not called to marriage. Both marriage and celibacy are gifts from God. If we were all called to celibacy, then all humanity would probably cease to exist, nowadays maybe not. There is so much pro-creation outside of marriage. There are many single Christians who struggle with self-control. Many single Christians are frustrated and impatient. Single Christians do not realize what they can do while being single in reference to ministry (I Corinthians 7:7). I am not saying that single people cannot marry. The call to single life is a gift. Patience is a virtue along with temperance.

I am not really a political person, but an independent, free-spirited person. I am learning to submit to the chain of command. I must learn first to serve before even becoming a priest or deacon. I must say that I might pursue the deaconate ministry. I was told by some Fire Baptized Holiness, one of the African American Pentecostal Group pastors, that I would make a great deacon. In the Baptist denomination I grew up in taught, the deacons were to be married. I am not certain if it is in the Baptist bylaws or not.

I am a steward. I have always served rather than led in the clerical sense. All my life, I have always been to myself. I have hardly had any relationships, only a little romance. The signs of celibacy were there, but I had not yet conquered my desires. Paul did say that, if a person burns with lust, it is better to marry than it is to burn (I Corinthians 7:9). Paul must have been a strong apostle when it came to desires. What human being has no sexual thoughts? Paul probably struggled with the call to celibacy. What about Jesus? Jesus knew that he was called to celibacy.

I remembered reading assignments on homosexuality in the pastoral office. There were some liberal scholars who argued that Jesus wrestled with sexual desires. No question that he was tempted, yet he did not fall into temptation. Jesus occupied the celibate call. The Bible does not specify the types of temptations that Jesus experienced, except the forty days in the wilderness (Matthew 4). True, Jesus prayed in the garden of Gethsemane to take the cup from him (John 17). Jesus rebuked Peter saying, "Get behind me Satan." He was constantly tempted, but for him to be tempted in the way we are tempted does not mention that he struggled with sexual desires. It does not mean that he didn't. There are Gnostic gospels which mention that Jesus and Mary Magdalene had something going on. The Synoptic gospels do mention that He was tempted with power in the political sense. The prayer Jesus prayed was to remain obedient to the will of the Father. Jesus was destined to suffer for the sins of humanity.

The other Apostles might have wrestled with the call to celibacy. Peter was believed to have been married. There was no actual proof apart from Paul's calling that all the Apostles were married. Luke 9:62 says that one of the disciples said that he would follow Jesus, but he must kiss or say good-bye to his home. Jesus told him "once he puts his hand into the plow and turns back is not fit for the kingdom" (NKJV). The disciple call to celibacy had already begun. The passage does not say if he was married or not. We know Timothy, Mark, Titus, Silas, and Luke were not married (Acts 15: 37-38). However these men devoted their lives to the ministry as single men. Stephen was a deacon, most likely not married. Elisha was not married when God called him to be a prophet, so was Jeremiah (I Kings 19:20). John the Baptist was not married. God did not prohibit marriage for all his prophets and apostles. Bishops and deacons did marry according to I Timothy 2, or Paul would not have written the letter giving Timothy the requirements for the call of the governing offices.

When I was a child, I had a passion for world geography because I went with my parents most of the time on vacations. I always desired, in my lifetime, to travel. No doubt that traveling is in my calling. I can see the world without being distracted with family. Maybe God intended for me not to marry during this present time. Who was to say? Definitely, I was far from ready for marriage. In a way, I feel free and happy as a single man because I am not tied down to marital commitment and have more time for God and my calling. One woman from Iowa said to me at the Steubenville Conference that the reason I have wrestled within my soul was that God was calling me to priesthood. No doubt that I am called to the priesthood, but I am not sure that I am called to be a Catholic priest because I believe that my calling will be a family priesthood call. My family was not Catholic. I came from a family of priests, and my family was anointed by God to perform such ministerial tasks. This does not mean that I will leave Catholicism because I have found a place where I can explore truth. I always believed that my calling will be greater than the confines of the Protestant Churches and the Catholic Churches. I would like to preach the gospel cross-culturally. However, I am not certain that one day I may or may not marry. Time will tell.

Chapter Fifteen
Urgent Evangelization from Within

IN MODERN-DAY CHRISTIANITY, THERE ARE many prodigal sons and daughters. The Church is filled with many prodigals. A prodigal is a backslider. A backslider is one who has fallen astray from both the faith and the fold. The prodigal is already in the family of God that needs to be restored back to the father. Before Jesus went to the world, He first preached to His own. The prodigal son represents Israel. Jesus used the parable of the lost sheep. If there were one hundred sheep in the fold, and one went astray, the shepherd goes and searches for the one to bring him back to the fold (Luke 15:11-32).

Even I, as a sheep, have wandered from the fold. When one wanders from the fold, then that sheep is unguarded, and it becomes prey for the wolves. Like the prodigal son, I came to my senses. The sheep have to be under watchful care. The pastors are the watchers over the sheep. I was not so far out there that I needed a preacher to bring me back into the fold. A little word to stand on is better than no word to stand on. Many Christians are the seeds that have been sown on rocky ground and on thorns. Either the seed never took on root, or the thorns have choked the life out of them. The wayside represents those who could not care less about the gospel because these people never allowed it to take root in their lives. So the enemy steals them. The destruction of many believers spiritually is the lack of knowledge.

The preacher is one who proclaims, not necessarily just a clergyman, but a layman. The offices were given by the Holy Spirit to edify and equip the laity for the work (Ephesians 4:11). Without souls, whether lost or found, there can be no evangelism. Like a business without customers cannot stay in business. The souls are why we are called to the fields. The harvest is plenty, but the laborers are few. As I said earlier, many Catholics did not know their Bible. Many Evangelicals did not know their Bible either.

Many Evangelicals and some Protestants preach the gospel with aggression. Catholics are strong on charity and social evangelism, but Protestants preached Jesus Christ directly from the Scriptures to the people out in the world. Catholics are not as aggressive. I struggled with Calvinism because of its doctrine of election. Calvinism made me think. I have to admit that evangelism was frustrating, especially in the modern culture. It seemed that the gospel was ineffective in reaching folk. There are so many obstacles and barriers that we face in our modern culture. In our culture, there is an increase in moral decline. Paul said, in the last days, that there will be a great falling away (apostasy). When a minister preaches about Jesus, there are people who still feel hopeless and useless. Pessimism sets in. Paul wrote of evangelism, saying that he was beaten and persecuted, yet he was persistent in his mission. It was obvious that the power of God (Holy Spirit) rested upon the apostles and the early Church. Why does there seems to be very little evidence of the Holy Spirit today? Evangelism is like talking to a brick wall nowadays.

Calvinists seemed to have a sound argument. It was very hard debating against Calvinists because of their highly academic theological skills. "Limited Atonement is 'limited' in that Christ's blood is shed for a limited number of people (the elect). It is not limited in its effectiveness for those people, but rather guarantees their salvation"[79] This was one of the reasons why I did not become a Presbyterian and a Calvinist. I, at one time, thought of myself as a four-point Calvinist rather than a five-point Calvinist. Most Christian groups disagree with Calvinist's view of salvation. Calvinists professors taught me that the gospel was preached to all, but Spirit speaks to only a few. Unless the Spirit draws him, he cannot come. Christ came to lay down His life for His sheep (John 10). I hardly saw any Catholics preaching like Jehovah's Witnesses or Mormons, by means of knocking on doors, going house to house to share the gospel. The Bible said to preach among the country sides by spreading the gospel. It is good to do what Jesus commanded of His disciples in the sense of virtue, but the message must be preached to the people outside the Church [walls].

Curtis Martin made some excellent points on the goal of evangelism. He said that the goal of evangelism is to introduce someone to Jesus Christ and to the Church. We also are to share how Jesus continues His saving presence on earth through His mystical body, the Church.[80] All Churches agree with this. Theologies often get in the way when it comes to evangelization.

Here is Curtis Martin's (Catholic author) response: "Many Catholics are not comfortable as evangelists. In our modern world, we are trained to live and let live, not to impose our views on others… Catholics don't believe that Jesus is God only for Christians; we must believe that He is God period."[81] According to my experiences, it is true, that not all churches preach Jesus's divinity, which is against the objective truth of the CHURCH!

---

79 Alexander J. Renullt. Reconsidering the Tulip. 2010. 73
80 (Scott Hahn & Regis Flaherty, 2004). 146-147
81 (Scott Hahn & Regis Flaherty, 2004). Ibid. 147

Of course, not all Christians are going to agree with one objective truth in reference to the Catholic Church, especially when the Church has corrupted itself and claims to be the objective truth. Protestants have done the same. There are dangers in both objective and subjective truth. Humans are creatures that are limited in understanding. Christians, let us admit that we do not know everything, that we know only in part! When we evangelize, we must not make our subjective truths norms for others. It is hard to preach objective truth when we are not certain if it is the whole truth. True, I can agree with this statement because of the thousands of sect interpretations, and many of them are personal interpretations and subjective truths. No prophecy of God has given man any private interpretation. Every Church group uses this passage to support their doctrines. Each sect claims to preach the objective truth which is their faith and the word of God. True, many dogmas can confuse people. Expressing the gospel is far more effective than preaching it. Any world religion can do the same. Jesus Christ must be known to the world through both word and deed.

Deception is not so much a group's dogma, but deception is really the interior motive in why a group evangelizes. Jesus said to the religious leaders that they went out into the world (Mediterranean World) getting converts and making them twice the hell as they were. The devil has his apostles converting people through false gospels.

I do believe that a person of the faith can lose his soul if not careful. Some denominations argue that one can lose his salvation. Some sects argue that a person is incapable of losing his soul because that individual was sealed by the Holy Spirit. Just because we believers were sealed for the day of redemption, that does not meant that we are never exempt from temptation or incapable of being susceptible to backsliding or apostasy. Keep in mind that salvation is another word for freedom. Yes, it true that the mandate is to proclaim the gospel to all the world and make disciples. It is true that we are trying to win as many souls to Christ as possible. However, we are to win souls to Christ without losing our own. We can be so caught up in preaching Jesus that we forget to nourish our own souls. The real evangelization begins from within. I agree with the Catholic view on evangelization. How can we be truly liberated, if we are not wise to salvation through the word of God? Every Church needs evangelization from within. We must be equipped for not only spiritual warfare, but for service in the sense of humility. Evangelism is not self-centeredness, but it serves as a cause that is outside of ourselves. We must be stable in our faith before going out to be missionaries for Christ. Evangelism means unwavering faith.

The whole point of "New Evangelization" is not only saving souls, but those who are saved and being saved can be spiritually cultivated in the faith. The knowledge of God is revealed only to the people of God because God's people are part of His covenant. If a person is in the family of God, then he or she will have a prudent and applicable understanding of God's truth. The knowledge that believers attain is through the spiritual marriage with Christ. New Evangelization means walking with God in fellowship.

There are three "Indicators of Vitality," according to Cardinal Donald Wuerl. The first indicator is the vitality of is parishes. The parish cultivates and equips its members to become agents of the New Evangelization. The parish helps its members to be effective in the community life, worship, education, service, and administration (Ezekiel 34:16). The second indicator of vitality is education: Catholic schools, elementary schools and religious education programs serve as the means of enriching and edifying the Catholic community. The final indicator is administration which means stewardship, leadership, management, and the decision-making process of the parish.[82] Paul used an illustration of the human body to explain its operation and infrastructure under the ministry of the Holy Spirit. Each member must understand its function within the body and how to be connected to the other members in order to be a healthy and effective organism and organization (1 Corinthians 12).

The Evangelicals' hearts were in the right place, and they have a burning zeal for winning souls. I will give the Evangelicals their props. The problem was that there was spiritual immaturity among many Evangelicals. Some Evangelicals (and I was an Evangelical) believe that knowledge was not necessary because all that was to be preached was faith alone. A person is not saved by knowledge indeed, but a person can perish without it.

True, works alone are not enough. Faith is valid when works are manifested. Both coincide and work cohesively. The world will watch us to see if we are living what we preach. Catholics are strong in active work, as well as many Evangelicals. Remember that all of our evangelization is through love. Love is more than just doing; it is being. Love is a nature, as well as an expression. Without love, we are nothing (1 Corinthians 13). Love is not vain. Love is what we are to proclaim, as well as express to the world. Many folk have been hurt by Church folk, and folk have resented not so much Jesus Christ Himself for the most part, but how He is displayed politically and religiously. If the Church does not proclaim with an apostolic spirit that the apostles had, then all the world would see its hypocrisy. Although we are not perfect people, we evaluate ourselves daily so that people may see the Jesus in us.

There was a book called Gandhi on Christianity. I remembered reading Gandhi's reason for converting to Christianity. Gandhi saw Christianity as no different from the Hindu religion. Gandhi had the

---

82 Cardinal Donald Wuerl, (New Evangelism, 2013). 66-67

deepest respect for Christianity. Gandhi saw the way of Jesus as the way of the Satyagraha (love force). Gandhi saw indifference. He saw the prejudices and the caste system in Christianity. Christians were not truly following the way of Christ. This is why many people refuse to convert or return to the Church.

The Church today finds itself compromising in the modern-day culture. This is why there is call for the new evangelization. There are so many Christians getting caught up in the New Age and Rationalism Humanism way of thinking. Spiritual maturity is necessary so that we will not be tossed to and fro by the very wind of doctrine (Ephesians 4:14). I speak from experience when it comes to falling into false doctrines. Timothy and Titus's task was to establish order as evangelists in Ephesus and Crete (1Timothy 1:3-5; Titus 1:5). Paul sowed the seeds of the gospel.

In the works of Dom Jean-Bapiste Chautard, he wrote that it was essential to nurture the life of Christ in us. Chautard said: "The interior life, far from being an easy life, is really a very laborious life. It is the source of devotedness, of incomparable activity. Because it is more the direct road to heaven, the saying of Jesus Christ that the kingdom of Heaven suffereth violence, and the violence bear it away, is applied to it in a special manner."[83] In other words, the internal life must be seen. Evangelism is seeing the good work which is internal so that God may be glorified. No internal manifestation means no impact through means of evangelism.

To be the universal sacrament of salvation, the Church must be true to its essential missionary nature. We are all apostles in a sense of missionaries, not the office of an apostle. The heart of the good news

---

83 Dom Jean-Baptiste Chautard. Inner Strength for the Active Apostles. How to Win Souls without Losing Your Own. (Manchester, New Hampshire: Sophia Institute Press, 2003). 22, Matthew 11:12, 33.

is found the kerygma (a central message proclaimed by the apostles on Pentecost Sunday) (Acts 2:14-41). In order to be the believable symbol of Christ, we must live out the message.[84]

---

[84] (Michael Pennock, 1998) 103. CCC 767-768: 849-854.

Chapter Sixteen
Catholic Cultural Shock

ONE OF THE MOST FASCINATING things about Catholicism is its cultural versatility and ethnicity. During the RCIA, the priest explained how open Catholicism is to different cultures and races. I am not saying that Catholicism has it all together when it comes to race and cultural relations, but it has a whole lot more to offer than Protestantism. There is far more segregation in Protestantism than in Catholicism. What I mean is that, there are black churches, white churches, Hispanic churches, and Asian churches that differ from one another in their forms of worship, music, and liturgy. Catholicism does have Spanish, English, Latin, and Asian Masses. I asked my parish priest, why don't we have an African-American Mass? The priest replied, "We do." I told him that I meant that the music worship in itself is not from my observation. The choir sings gospel songs, but no one really claps. It is a multi-cultural Catholic Church. Is it natural that we are different? That is what makes the Church so unique.

The Mass is bone-dry, I told the priest, and he agreed. My definition of African-American Mass was singing, shouting, and lifting up hands. The Church setting I grew up in was more ecstatic (Charismatic). Music is the center in many African-American Churches because the music uplifts the spirit. I learned from my African-American United Methodist "Black Studies" professor that black people worshipped God through experience, human suffering, and oppression. There are some Black

Catholic churches that do get down, but not in that area. Sometimes I get homesick because I sometimes long for the music. Music is the means through which many Churches express themselves to God, along with preaching. My parish Church has a rich black history.

The Spanish Masses are rich in Spanish and Latino culture, along with the Spanish language. I found the Spanish Masses to be more exciting than the English Masses. The Spanish-speaking people do get down when it comes to music. Although I do not know Spanish, I am intrigued with the songs sung in Spanish. The Spirit knows what my spirit is uttering. As God's people of many kindred and tongues, we worship God in Spirit and in truth. That is the sign of the true worshipper (John 4:24).

Everyone is not the same. I became more open to ethnicity when I went with a Jewish classmate to a Messianic synagogue. At first, I did not understand the Jewish customs and order of worship. I had learned to step out of the Baptist mode a long time ago. The Jewish people opened their arms to me, and I learned to fellowship with Jews and respect their customs. Two of my positive qualities are adapting and blending in with people who are different from me.

In Catholicism, there is a melting pot of national and international ethnic groups that see themselves as one big Catholic family. I admit that Catholicism is not perfect. There are some prejudices, especially in America, mainly in the south. I cannot say this for the whole world because I have not been around the world to make such comments. I grew up in the south. Definitely the South still has "the Jim Crow" spirit lingering within its churches. I had a black Methodist professor who quoted a famous saying: "The most segregated day of the week is Sunday." This statement is very true in America no matter who said this statement. The North has the same problem. After all, this is America! America has come a long way, but she still has a very long way to go. I visited "non-denominational" church that claimed not to be religious but spiritual, not traditional but contemporary. The Bible College that I attended was inter-denominational, but rooted in Wesleyan and Pentecostal doctrines. The students were from different countries. I liked the fact that students from other countries prayed and praised God in the same setting. Even though there was a racial melting pot in the school, but to grow and love in unity was far from that. I can say that Mega churches have the right idea for integrating races and praising in an interracial setting. Yet, the churches have social-class divisions in them like the denominations and Catholics do. My whole point is that no church, not even the Catholic Church, is perfect. The Holy Spirit was sent to not only equip the Catholic community spiritually, but to perfect her virtually.

I have been to a few Catholic churches in my area. I have been to a couple of Catholic churches that I felt were very racist. I have been to a couple of Catholic churches that had hardly had any African-Americans in them. I saw more Hispanics. I knew that there were black Catholic churches. I was not so not naïve as to not think that prejudice exists in the black churches, too! I have been in Protestant churches where I have had some whites staring me down during the whole service, and there are some blacks who do the same towards some whites. I learned to embrace the fact that people are human and subject to error. There are good people in the churches, and they love God. There were some good, down-to-earth black and white churches around. There were some white churches, and especially black churches as a whole, that will extend their arms to all races.

One of the things African- American churches and Catholics do have in common is fighting against oppression. The Catholics have always defended those ethnic groups worldwide who suffer from different forms of tyranny. James Cone, a black author and theologian, wrote a book called God of the Oppressed. Cone's works centered on how God and

Jesus related to black people. His works were very controversial to some, but his points are clear. God was on the side of the oppressed.

When it comes to world religions, Catholics are very open. In Catholicism pluralism is the belief that one is open to embracing truths or element of truths in every religion without converting to them. In the denominations, it is Sola Scripture (Scripture Alone). Many non-Catholic Christians would bash out another's religion by beating someone upside the head with the Bible. I have seen this happen in the Prison Ministry. The chaplains always told the different church groups not to impose their religion on the inmates, and condemned the inmates. I have observed Christian groups in the laundromats, the grocery store, the restaurants, and even on the main street sidewalks, preaching hellfire and brimstone, which has nothing wrong with it, except one eternally condemns a person abruptly because of his cradle-faith. Catholicism has a very high respect for Islam and Judaism. Catholics do respect Buddhism and Hinduism and other world religions. I could say that the religion with the strongest virtues outside of Christianity that I observed was Islam, especially the Nation of Islam better known as the Fruit of Islam. Islam is a religion with strong disciplines. I have encountered this religion from experience. Judaism is second. Many of these religions have virtues and disciplinary and dietary laws. Paul said that there are those who have the form of godliness, but deny the power thereof. Denying the power thereof means that those groups denied the authority and the source who is God the Father and Jesus Christ.

Pluralism in the Evangelical circles means that all religions lead to God which was rejected. Both Catholics and Protestant-Evangelical groups reject relativism. Our modern-day culture embraces relativism, which teaches there is no absolute truth. Some Christian groups are exclusive, and some are inclusive. Catholicism is open to truths that are universal, but do not embrace syncretism (combining world religions).

Catholicism respects each entity. Christianity is the only faith that teaches Jesus Christ which is Absolute Truth. I cannot deviate from my position on Jesus as the Truth, the Way, and the Life. No man can come to the Father except through Him (John 14:6). Jesus was not referring to organizations in particular. Jesus was referring to sin itself that kept humanity distant from God through Adam's disobedience. Jesus was the only way back to God's presence. There is no way around it. How can we have that perfect communion with God the Father without the Son and the Holy Spirit? The objective and focus is Christian unity within the Body of Christ. No doubt that the Church is visible as well as invisible (spiritually). Since we are visible to the world, then the world is our neighbor. The Church serves as the beacon of light to the world as Jesus was the light in the world. How can the world, filled with diverse cultures and religions, see the light of God and glorify the Heavenly Father, if the Church, Christianity, as a whole entity does not express that light?

Here was the common ground between the Protestant and Catholics! Both objected to the cultural immorality in the modern-day society. Both protested against unethical issues such as abortion, contraband, contraception, euthanasia, and same-sex marriage. It means that people who advocate such controversial issues often feel discriminated against or hated. I have met folk that use this as a so-called hate crime, especially those who fit in these unethical categories. Christians often get attacked by certain groups because Christians protest against such issues. The first reaction is "This is a hate crime." Christians are not closed-minded. Christianity is often accused as being judgmental and closed-minded. Christianity is social. Christianity addresses, not only the social concerns, but economic concerns. Christianity serves as the moral conscience to the world. Catholicism very strongly arouses the moral conscience of the world governments. Both Protestants and Catholics do seek and win new souls. The Great Commission is the ultimate objective for the Church to carry out (Matthew 28:28).

Much of Catholicism's teachings are based on the letter of James because of faith and work, not merit salvation. No man can merit salvation on mere works. Pure Religion is serving our fellowman (James 1:26). Pure Religion means feeding the hungry, clothing the naked, defend the poor, and so on. WWJD (What Would Jesus Do?) sums up in a nutshell what Jesus expects from His disciples? The Father cannot be glorified unless people see both our good works, and let our light shine (Matthew 5:16). The Church is not saved on mere virtues, but our virtues can win the world over to Jesus Christ.

I talked to some Catholics, especially a couple of black Catholics who had been Catholic for a while. One person, who was black, told me that the main reason he converted to Catholicism was because of its involvement in the community. My favorite Catholic is Saint Francis of Assisi. Saint Francis of Assisi exemplified what Jesus commanded the Church to do with humility. The Franciscan Catholic Church that I attend is rooted in Afro-American culture and heritage. I never objected to culture and ethnicity, but rather the behavior that we have toward one another. We can attend the same Church, and we can grow together as one community spiritually. The Jewish people told me that they grow, suffer, and think together as a community. This was Paul's objective goal in his letters. The objective is to become One New Man. Prejudice is not new, and neither is racism. This goes back to the beginning since the fall of man. It's part of the fallen human nature. In Paul's time, there was prejudice. The Jews had issues with the Samaritans, not because of color, but because of religion and customs. We must be careful not to put customs above God. Jesus said that God is Spirit and they that worship must worship him in spirit and in truth. Jesus was color-blind, status-blind, and gender-blind. He came to those who were in need of a physician.

Jesus served as our example (Philippians 2:6-9). He was the epitome of righteousness. Catholicism taught me to put other's needs above my own. Catholicism does not discriminate against race, color, sex, age, national origin or religion. Evangelicals always use the abbreviation "WWJD" (What Would Jesus Do?). The two greatest commandments Jesus told His disciples was to "love God and thy neighbor." My parish priest uses the illustration of the cross. The love between God and man is vertical, and the love between the neighbors is horizontal. The question is: who is thy neighbor? As I said in chapter two, it is not just me and Jesus, but me and my neighbor. If I do not love my brother, then the light is not in me (1 John 4:20). Jesus said that the second commandment is to love your neighbor as yourself (Mark 12:31).

At the Steubenville Bible Conference at Franciscan University, there was a sense of family in the atmosphere. I saw far more genuine unity among Catholics from the north than from the Catholics of the south. I am a Southerner, born and raised. The south has been known for segregation. No doubt the north has segregation as well. The conference consisted of ethnic groups from all over the country and parts of the world. In the covenantal body, we are no longer foreigners (Ephesians 2:19). It is possible to achieve the one household that Paul spoke of in Ephesians5: 21-33-6:9.

I confess that I would have a hard time returning to Protestantism. One day I may have to go back to Protestantism, but not as a Protestant. There are things that I feel led to share. When I was a Protestant, the time was not right. There is strong segregation in the churches. Some Evangelicals are waking up to the fact that the Church sects are divided spiritually, racially, and culturally. The melancholy in the Church body is division. The word melancholy means "depressing, tragedy, or sadness." For example, we are not to grieve the Holy Spirit, but we do when we fight among each other by creating walls of division. Anyone can assemble. Can we reason together? Obviously, there is division. The sadness is not assembling together as one body, but growing in unity as one. Are we able to suffer as one body? Are we able to stick together in the thick and the thin? We are different culturally, but not spiritually. Before there can be cultural and racial unity, there has to be spiritual unity within the body of Christ. How can the Church unite a world, when it cannot unite itself? Once we can deal with the Jim Crow spirit of division, then the Church can make progress in what Christ has called her to do.

I grew up in an African-American Baptist setting. The only religious world I knew was the African-American cultural setting. When I attended a small interdenominational Bible College, I was exposed to the different nationalities. It was a cultural shock for me. I learned more about Africa from African Bible students than I did through public school. I made friends with students from Romania, Russia, Vietnam, Kenya, Ethiopia, South Africa, Liberia, India, the Dominican Republic, and Trinidad. I was amazed with the cultures that made me interested in world religions and cultures. I went with a Jewish classmate to a Messianic Synagogue. It astounded me in how different the style of worship and customs were from where I came from.

When I attended an Associate Reformed Seminary, I was exposed to the different denominational settings and formalities. Each had its own tradition. I was exposed to pluralism which enabled me to comprehend cultural, political, and religious tolerances that impacted our American culture. Seminary revealed to me how divided we were as a people of God and as a country. I took classes on how Church leaders could interact in a pluralistic society without offending different faiths. When 9/11 occurred, there were many emotional reactions among students. Islam was the most talked about religion at that time. There was much hatred toward the group of people blamed for the event. When I attended a technical school that had a teaching on Islam, there were people interested in taking courses on religions and culture. I never signed up for it. America is no longer black and white, but she is now a melting pot nation filled with many customs, ethnic groups, religions, and cultures. Actually God was setting me up for Catholicism which is a melting pot of cultures and nationalities. I needed to be open-minded, yet Catholicism remained true to her faith without compromising.

Unity, not fusion, is the objective goal for the Church Body. Syncretism is dangerous. Each religion has to remain its own individual entity. It will cause great confusion and chaos. Religion should not be a melting pot. I agree with Mahatma Gandhi to a certain extent. Gandhi was not Christian. All religions were true according to Gandhi. All religions were branches from the same tree. Religions have different roads, and there is no need for all to travel the same road.[85] This is contrary to what Jesus said. Jesus said that He is the way back to the Father. The narrow way leads to eternal life. Gandhi defined religion (religio) as "to bind" or "bind together." Gandhi said that religion was not to bring division but unity in terms of people.[86] Gandhi did not believe in religious conversion. Gandhi thought that convincing a person to convert from one religion to another was being mischievous and pointless, yet coercive. True the conversion is not done by human agency, if being, but by God himself.[87] It is the Holy Spirit who is the

---

85 Robert Ellsberg. Gandhi on Christianity. (Mary Knoll, NY: Orbis Books, 1991). 80-81
86 Ibid., 89
87 Ibid. 86-87

Agent of soul conversion. The Church serves as the visible instrument in which the Holy Spirit manifests himself. He considered "real conversion" as being a better person regardless of one's faith. Religion was not to be a caste pyramid divided into groups. Catholic unity is not to syncretize religions, but to respect each of the truths in them which are universal, except that the other world religions do not have Jesus Christ.

Mahatma Gandhi made an excellent point. Gandhi said: "All faiths constitute a revelation of Truth, but all are imperfect and liable to error. Reverence for other faiths need not blind us to their faiths. Religions are not revealed full blown from heaven. They are human responses to the glimpses of God's revelation, human creations, bearing the imprint of inevitable human imperfections. Religions are not 'the Truth,' though they aim us towards the Truth."[88] What the Church speaks might be infallible, but inerrant it might not be. Pluralism means sharing in a society politically, culturally, and religiously. Pluralism is living within a society that tolerates differences in ethnicity, philosophy, and religion. Pluralism involves horizontal unity among neighbors. The Church's call is to spread the good news and love of Jesus Christ to the world through virtue. The Pope is the strong figure that brings people into unity, not in the New World Order sense, but in the sense of building a bond within humanity. When I was a Protestant, I was taught that Christianity did not embrace pluralism because it was believed to have a belief which says "all religions lead to God." We have no right to bash out any religion because it is not a Christ-centered religion. All religions do not lead to God, but they all have some element of truth. Catholicism does not deny that Jesus is the Way to Salvation, according to Catholic dogmas.

---

88 Ibid. 81

Reflections

In the beginning, I had resentment toward organized religion. Paul said to the Church of Corinth that God was a God of order. The whole purpose of the Catholic journey was to connect with God by being in His presence, especially in the Mass and the Rosary. In the Catholic Faith, I felt connected to God. Whenever I went to another Church to visit, it was not the same. The essence of God seemed to have been at the places of Christian sects. I could say how far the Catholic faith has taken me spiritually. She, the Mother Church, has helped me to see my internal soul status and deal with it with God's help. There is no doubt that the Holy Spirit is with the Catholic Church. The Catholic Church has many issues within herself to deal with. I feel that had I returned to Protestantism or the Baptist denomination, I would be so inwardly dismantled that I probably would have gone astray. I have come close to apostasy, but I fear the Lord and his judgment far more. I felt that I had to seek refuge in a place where I could heal and grow in spiritual enrichment. Ever since I became Catholic, the people of my former faith seem to have alienated themselves from me. I never wanted to disconnect myself from those I knew. My mission was to make the connection with the Creator Himself.

Catholicism is more than just a religious belief system. Catholicism is a spiritual family. In Catholicism, there were some Catholics who never made me feel welcome to the family. In Catholicism, I pursued truth, purpose, and discernment, yet I felt dormant in ministerial involvement. This made me question my place in Catholicism. There were times I felt that I needed to leave Catholicism, but where else would I go?

The words of one of the Catholic sisters in the bookstore echo back to me often. concerning the coming persecution of the Church.

Catholicism is the only place where I could gear up for the upcoming persecution. I plan to study the Book of Revelation in depth. I believe that the Catholic Church will play a major role in the end times.

I love the new pope, Pope Francis. I was watching carefully to see if he was the final pope according to Saint Malachy's prophecy. This brought major concerns. I questioned some of dispensational futuristic teachings on the end times such as the pre-rapture (rapture before the tribulation), which was never Catholic teaching. I found that out on my conference trip. I did struggle with Catholicism's rejection of a literal future millennium reign of Christ. I do stand on Matthew 24, in which Jesus spoke on the Great Tribulation. The Holy Spirit will reveal all this to me in due time.

I believe that the True Church will stand in the evil tribulation times. Matthew 16:18 will be the fulfillment of the prophecy that the gates of hell will not prevail against the Church of Jesus Christ. Although the Catholic Church has withstood the times and has a far more rich history that the Protestant churches, the Church will stand not because of its rich treasures, arts, and history. The Church will stand because of its foundation because she, the Church, is the ground and pillar of truth (1 Timothy 3:15). I understood that Jesus told Peter that His Church would be built upon the Revelation of God (Matthew 16:18). Christ is the Revelation of God (Revelation 22:13). Peter was the builder of Christ's Church, along with the apostles. The Church has done battle, and she does battle until the end. In the tribulation, the kingdom of God will suffer violently and the violence takes it by force, but she will prevail against the gates of hell (Matthew 11:12).

In conclusion, Catholicism must be highly respected for preserving many of the Christian traditions through arts and symbols. After all, most the Christian groups were from her offspring, but all Christianity, including Catholicism was the offspring of Judaism. True followers of Christ are those who act on and keep his commandments. The label does not make the faith true. Pure religion, as James mentioned, is the expression of God's love (James 1:26). Therefore, a dead faith is a faith that does not express the love and righteousness of God into the world. Jesus has already explained the true marks of a believer through His teachings and parables. After reading this book on Catholicism's beliefs, one should now have a basic understanding of the faith. I took a class on Lumen Gentium (Latin meaning "In light of Nations") which enabled me to excavate the spirit of Catholic traditional teachings.

My favorite part of the book is Chapter Twelve: Catholic Meditations & Acts of Contrition. After confirmation my spiritual growth began with Catholic meditations and Acts of Contrition, I began soul-searching rather than seeking abstract theological knowledge. The word for growth in the Greek is auxano and that means to increase. Every aspect of the believers' lives is to go through the cultivation process. My objective was to not only make the connection with the Lord, but to be made free inwardly. Walking with God meant more to me than any theological truths. What good is theology without the relationship with the Lord? Theology should be the basic fundamental principles of salvation since the Scriptures make one wise unto salvation. One cannot walk in something that he or she does not know. The objective of the Catholic journey is to make peace with ourselves. Sister Kathryn James Hermes book, Making Peace with Yourself, inspired me to make peace with myself. With all the knowledge I have attained, I never learned to let go. Self can become our obstacle. Holding in unforgiveness and past hurts not only stagnates the soul, but also becomes detrimental to the soul because the soul is a living delicate being that can become fragile if we allow it. Sister Kathryn James Hermes said, "The only way I can keep accepting the present moment, asking Jesus just to be with me."[89] In other words it is about letting go and letting

---

[89] Kathryn James Hermes. Making Peace with Yourself. (Boston, MA: Pauline Books Media, Daughters of Saint Paul, 2007). 114

God. The focus is the present, because it is a gift from God. Do deal with the present by learning to make peace with God and self. Some groups I was taught in used the term works righteousness, which means that salvation is merited through human efforts. Salvation has nothing to do with meriting righteousness of God because it is Christ's merits and not our own. We are to take responsibility for our actions. The calling of every believer is to worship God and to humble oneself for service and devotion (Romans 12:2). Everyone is called for something in life. The Christian is called to conform into image of Christ.

I know that I have a long way to go before I can call myself a Catholic apologist (defender of the Catholic Faith). I am on the long life journey of learning. Catholicism is not the end for me. The goal is to become human like Christ was on earth. The virtues of the Spirit help me to become humane, as Christ was. The journey is to go from irrational to rational. We take on the mind of Christ. We can never be divine in the sense of becoming God, but we can become spiritually human in the likeness of Christ. Jesus was the definition of human. In this life, our spiritual journey is to become transformed into the likeness of Christ daily. The believer's journey does not end at confession during an altar call service. Cultivation is a must. God is cultivating us daily. Therefore, there is no room for complacency or idleness. Spiritual growth is a means to strive toward the mark. Catholicism is a continuation of the spiritual journey I began a long time ago.

In the name of the Father, the Son and the Holy Spirit (Sign of the Cross), May God Bless You, Keep You, and Enrich You! Amen.

Bibliography

Abel, Robert. The Healing Power of Jesus. (Denver, CO: Valentine Publishing Co., 2006)

Abel, Robert. The Catholic Warrior. (Denver CO: Valentine Publishing Co.,2004)

Abbot Vonier. A Key to the Doctrine of the Eucharist. (Bethsada, MD: Zaccheus Press, 2003).

Apostoli, Andrew. When God Asks for an Undivided Heart, Choosing Celibacy in Love and Freedom. (Irving, TX: Basilica Press, 2007).

Boer, Harry R. A Short History of the Early Church. (Grand Rapids, MI: W.B. Eerdman's Publishing Company, 1976).

Bernard, Bangley. The Cloud of Unknowing. (Brewer, MA: Paraclete Press, 2006)

Boylan, M. Eugene. Difficulties in Mental Prayer. (Princeton, NJ: Scepter Press, 1997)

Catechism of the Catholic Church Second Edition, Promulgated by Pope John Paul II (Libertia Editrice Vaticana, 1994, 1997)

Cone, James H. God of the Oppressed. (New York, NY: Seabury Press, 1975)

Ellsberg, Robert. Gandhi on Christianity. (Mary Knoll, NY: Orbis Books, 1991)

Finley, James. Catholic Meditation. (New York, NY: Harper One Publishers, 2005)

Gill, Tom. Confessions. Saint Augustine. (Gainesville, Fl: Bridge-Logos, 2003).

Green, Thomas H. Weeds Among the Wheat. (Norte Dame, IN: Ave Maria Press, 1984)

Hahn, Scott, Flaherty, Regis J. Catholics for a Reason III Scripture and the Mystery of the Mass. (Steubenville, OH: Emmaus Road Publishing), 2004

Hermes, Kathryn James. Making Peace with Yourself. (Boston, MA: Pauline Books & Media, Daughters of Saint Paul, 2007).

Keaton, Karl. What Catholics Really Believe. 52 answer to Common Misconceptions about the Catholic Faith. (San Francisco, CA: Ignatius Press, 1992).

Jergens, William A. The Faith of the Fathers Volume 1. (Collegeville, MN: Liturgical Press, 1970).

Jergens, William A. The Faith of the Fathers Volume 2. (Collegeville, MN: Liturgical Press, 1979).

Jurgens, William A. The Faith of the Fathers Volume 3. (Collegeville, MN: Liturgical Prese, 1979).

John Paul II. God Father and Creator, Volume One. (Boston, MA: Pauline Books, Daughters of Saint Paul, 1996).

John Paul II. A Catechesis on Salvation History. The Trinity Embrace God's Saving Plan, Volume Six. (Boston, MA: Pauline Books & Media, Daughters of Saint Paul, 2002).

Keaton, Karl. What Catholics Really Believe. (San Francisco: Ignatius Press, 1992).

Longenecker, Dwight. More Christianity. (Huntington, IN: Our Sunday Visitor Publishing Division, 2002).

New American Standard Version. The Catholic Bible. (Oxford University Press, 2007, 2011),

New King James Version, 1982. Spirit Filled Life Bible. (Nashville: Nelson Publishers Co., 1991)

Pennock, Michael. This is Our Faith. (Norte Dame, IN: Ave Maria Press, 1998).

Renault, Alexander J. Reconsidering Tulip, 2010.

Richard, Thomas R. The Ordinary Path to Holiness. (Staten Island, NY: The Society of St Paul, 2003).

Richardson, Cyril. Early Christian Fathers. (New York: Collier Books, Macmillan Press, 1970).

Shea, Mark (Senior Editor of the Catholic Exchange). The DaVinci Deception. (West Chester, PA: Ascension Press, 2006).

Sheen, Fulton J. Way to Inner Peace. (New York, NY: Society of St. Paul, 1995)

Stackpole, Robert. Saint Peter Lives in Rome. (Stockbridge, MA: Marian Press, 2006).

Suprenant, Leon J. Catholic for a Reason II, Scripture and the Mystery of the Mother of God. (Steubenville, OH: Emmaus Book Publishing, 2000).

Waldstein, Michael. John Paul II, Man and Woman He Created Them, A Theology of the Body. (Boston, MA: Pauline Media Books, 2006).

Wuerl, Cardinal Donald. New Evangelism, Passing on the Catholic Faith Today. (Huntington, IN: Our Sunday Visitor Publishing Division, 2013).

www.ingramcontent.com/pod-product-compliance
Lightning Source LLC
Chambersburg PA
CBHW030325080526
44584CB00012B/713